Working with German

Level 1

Teacher's Book

Angela Embleton

Adviser to the project:
Peter Lupson

Stanley Thornes (Publishers) Ltd

First published in 1991 by:
Stanley Thornes (Publishers) Ltd
Ellenborough House
Wellington Street
CHELTENHAM GL50 1YUD

Reprinted 1993

British Library Cataloguing in Publication Data

Working with German: level 1: Teacher's Book
I. Title
438.3

ISBN 0-85950-839-0

Typeset by Tech-Set, Gateshead, Tyne and Wear.
Printed in Great Britain at Looseleaf, Wiltshire.

Contents

Introduction

The exercises in this book are intended solely for use with *Working with German Level 1*.

The notes for each chapter are divided into four sections:

1 Teacher's notes to help with lesson preparation for each chapter in the coursebook.
2 Aufgaben: These are intended to help consolidate the vocabulary and grammar points which occur in each chapter.
3 Role-play (Chapters 1–9): These pages should be divided in two when photocopied. Each student questions another student who has a different sheet. Students have the opportunity to play two roles:
   a) to seek and give information as an official (railway clerk, receptionist, doctor etc.)
   b) to seek and give information as a customer or client (passenger, hotel guest, patient etc.).
4 A list of the main vocabulary from each chapter.

Each of these four sections are grouped together in the book. To find a section relating to a particular chapter, see the contents list.

Teacher's Notes

Besuch aus Deutschland

Main vocabulary	Nationalities
	Professions
	Family members

Language	Verbs: **heißen, wohnen, arbeiten, sein,**
	haben, erwarten, kommen, buchstabieren
	The nominative case

Verbs

Use yourself as a model to introduce students to the verbs: heißen, wohnen, arbeiten, kommen (aus) (see page 2, exercise 1). Ask students: **Wie heißen Sie? Wo wohnen Sie?** etc. to elicit the correct responses. Students should then ask each other these questions.

Introduce **haben, sein:**
   Ich bin Lehrer(in).
   Ich habe zwei Kinder.

Explain the differences between **haben** and **sein** and the regular verbs. Make sure all students can say and ask the correct questions to elicit:
   Ich heiße _____ .
   Ich komme aus _____ .
   Ich bin _____ bei der Firma _____ .
   Ich wohne in _____ etc.

Use pictures of well-known people of different nationalities or write names on a card to explain:
   Er/sie kommt aus Italien.
   Er/sie ist Italiener(in).
Make sure students can answer and ask:
   Woher kommen Sie/kommt er? etc.

These pictures or names can also be used to extend knowledge of professions:
   Er ist Schauspieler, sie ist Sängerin.

The nominative case

Write up:

	Masculine	*Feminine*	*Neuter*
Nominative	der Mann	die Frau	das Kind
	ein	eine	ein

Explain the importance of learning the gender of any new noun. Explain that this case is used when the noun is the subject of the sentence. Those who have never studied another language may not be certain of the difference between the subject and the object. Give examples:
   Der Direktor arbeitet in London.
   Die Frau heißt Maria.

The accusative case

Point out that the sentence at the bottom of page 6 **Er hat auch** *einen* **Sohn und** *eine* **Tochter** contains two examples of the accusative case. There are more examples in the next chapter.

Kapitel 2

Wann fahren Sie?

Main vocabulary	Days of the week Months Numbers The time

Language	Separable verbs: **abholen, ankommen, weiterfahren, abfliegen** Modal verbs: **sollen, möchten** The future tense The accusative and dative cases

Time

Introduce smaller numbers using any reasonable visual aid. Write larger numbers on card or board.

Make flashcards to show (a) days of the week and (b) months of the year. Give today's date: *der* _____ *te* _____ . Then explain the difference in a sentence like: Ich habe *am* _____ *(s)ten* _____ Geburtstag.
Ask students the dates of their birthdays and then today's date.

Use a clock with movable hands to explain the time. Allow plenty of practice!

Explain the concept of modal verbs and separable verbs. To practise this, move the hands of the clock and ask:
Wann kommt er an?
Wann fliegt er ab?
Wann hole ich ihn ab?
Wann soll ich ihn abholen?

Use the days of the week flashcards as prompts to ask:
Wann möchte er kommen?
Möchte er am Freitag kommen?
Sollen wir ihn am Mittwoch erwarten?

Explain that using **werden** for the future tense has the same effect on the sentence as a modal verb.

The accusative case

Write up:

	Masculine	Feminine	Neuter		Masculine	Feminine	Neuter
Nominative	der	die	das		ein	eine	ein
Accusative	den	die	das		einen	eine	ein

There is a list of prepositions taking the accusative on page 24 of the coursebook, but **für** is the first one students meet. Practice: **für den Geschäftsführer, für das Kind, für die Frau.**

Make a list of some of the professions already introduced, e.g. **Sekretärin, Direktor, Lehrerin, Geschäftsführer** etc.
Teacher: Ist das für *die* Sekretärin?
Student: Nein, das ist für *den* Direktor etc.

4

Explain that even where no preposition requiring the accusative is present, it is always used to denote the object of the sentence.

Wir erwarten *den* Geschäftsführer.
Er hat *einen* Sohn.
Sie hat *eine* Tochter.

Make cards with brief details, e.g. **Hans Nieß – verheiratet – Sohn (Peter) – Tochter (Anna)**. Encourage students to describe the subject.

Er ist verheiratet.
Er hat einen Sohn und eine Tochter.
Der Sohn heißt Peter, die Tochter heißt Anna.

The dative case

Write the dative case on the board using the same format as for the other cases. Make it clear which prepositions can contract and which cannot.

Practise the dative using flashcards to show days, means of transport and places.

Herr Braun fährt _____ Montag _____ Zug _____ Messe.
Frl. Schmidt fährt _____ Donnerstag _____ Bahn _____ Flughafen.
Er holt sie um neun Uhr _____ Hotel/Flughafen/Messe/Bahnhof/Firma ab.

Word order

Use the flashcards to practise the same sentences but start each sentence with: **am Montag, um neun Uhr** etc.

Possessive adjectives

Write out the possessive adjectives on card or on the board. Explain that they behave exactly like **ein**. Practise the possessive adjectives by using your own and students family members as teaching aids.

Meine Tochter heißt . . .
Wie heißt *sein* Sohn?
Ihr Mann?
Kennen Sie *seinen* Sohn? etc.

Make up a small family tree and some information to go with it. Use pictures if possible, for example:

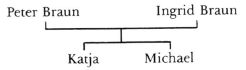

Peter spielt mit Michael Golf.
Peter geht mit Ingrid ins Theater.
Ingrid geht mit Katja ins Café.
Peter geht mit Michael und Katja schwimmen.

Ask questions:
Geht Peter mit seinen Kindern ins Theater?
Geht Ingrid mit ihrem Sohn ins Café? etc.

Kapitel 3

Unterwegs

| **Main vocabulary** | Train travel |
| | 24-hour clock |

Language	Modal verbs: **wollen, müssen, können**
	Separable verbs: **einsteigen, umsteigen**
	Personal pronouns
	The genitive case
	Verbs with the dative case

Timetables

Using a clock with movable hands, revise the time and extend it to the 24-hour clock.

Introduce: **Wann fährt der nächste Zug nach** _____? and **Wann kommt er in** _____ **an?** to help practise the 24-hour clock and to set the scene for the cassette conversation.

Make a card showing the symbols ⇌ and some prices to teach and practise einfach, hin und zurück, **Was kostet das? Erster oder zweiter Klasse?**

Make a second card showing a list of train destinations and, if applicable, where passengers should change. Use the list to teach and practise:
   Kann ich direkt nach _____ **fahren?**
   Nein, Sie müssen in _____ **umsteigen.**

Use the clock and _both_ cards to practise:
   Wohin möchten Sie fahren? Was kostet das hin und zurück? Wann fährt der nächste Zug? Wo muß ich umsteigen? etc.

Beamter appears on page 28. This is the first example of a weak noun so it provides a good opportunity to explain how weak nouns decline.

Personal pronouns

Write up the table of personal pronouns or refer students to page 40 of the coursebook.

Make cards with names, for example: Fräulein Schmidt, Herr Braun, Hans u. Maria, your name, your name and a friend's name, a student's name. Use the cards to build sentences practising personal pronouns.
   Frl. Schmidt kommt um zehn Uhr an. Herr Braun kommt um elf Uhr an.
   Er holt _sie_ **vom Bahnhof ab. Wir holen** _ihn_ **vom Bahnhof ab.** etc.

   Use the same cards to practise **danken** and **helfen**.
   Fräulein Schmidt hilft Ihnen.
   Sie danken _ihr/ihm_ etc.

The genitive case

Give examples:
   Montag ist der erste Tag _der_ **Woche.**
   Januar ist der erste Monat _des_ **Jahres.**
   Der Direktor _der_ **Firma.**
   Der Name _des_ **Hotels.**

Refer students to the list of prepositions on page 39. Ask them to work out how to say: within a week, outside the town, during the month, during his stay etc.

Kapitel 4

Unterkunft in Deutschland

Main vocabulary	Registering at a hotel
Language	Verbs: **ausfüllen, besichtigen, nehmen** The imperative Adjective agreement The comparative Demonstrative article

The imperative

Give some examples of the imperative using verbs that students have already learnt.
  Reservieren – Zimmer (Bitte reservieren Sie ein Zimmer)
  Kaufen – Fahrkarte
  Drücken – Taste
  Kommen – am Freitag
  Bleiben – bis Montag
  Empfehlen – mir ein Hotel
  Buchstabieren – Namen

Also give examples using separable verbs.
  Abholen – um neun Uhr (Holen Sie mich um neun Uhr ab)
  Einwerfen – das Geld
  Einsteigen – in den Zug
  Umsteigen – in Köln
  Ausfüllen – das Anmeldeformular

The comparative

Explain the formation of the comparative (see page 54 of the coursebook). Ask students to give the comparative of: schön, angenehm, klein, ruhig, teuer and freundlich (which all appear in Chapter 4 or earlier).

Adjective agreement

The first example of this in the text is on page 45, line two: eine herrliche Aussicht. However, I suggest you delay detailed explanations until at least the end of exercise 7 on page 50.

Make small cards showing: (a) die englische Verkaufsleiterin (b) das alte Büro (c) das moderne Büro (d) der neue Geschäftsführer.

The accusative case

Shuffle and deal out the cards face down. You or other students ask **Haben Sie den neuen Geschäftsführer?** etc.

The dative case

Position two cards one behind the other. Ask **Wo ist das alte Büro? Es ist hinter dem modernen Büro** etc. Also use the prepositions **vor, neben, gegenüber**.

Make a second set of cards depicting, for example: **ein großes Hotel, eine moderne Jugendherberge, ein kleiner Gasthof.** If you can draw characters to look as if they correspond to the pictures, you can ask **Wo wohnt er?** etc.

Further suggestions

Use pictures of people from catalogues. This does involve introducing vocabulary not yet covered in the coursebook, i.e. colours and articles of clothing, but this vocabulary can then be transferred to the students themselves.
　　Was trägt er/sie? Ein weißes Hemd, eine blaue Jacke etc.

Write up:

Das Hotel hat	große	Schwimmbad
	eine herrliche	Garten
	finnische	Zimmer
	ein modernes	Aussicht
	einen großen	Sauna
	ein gemütliches	Eßzimmer
	einen schönen	Parkplatz

Students should then match the adjectives to the appropriate nouns.

Kapitel 5

Essen und Trinken

Main vocabulary	Meeting people
	Ordering a meal in a restaurant

Language	The perfect tense
	Subordinate clauses

Perfect tense

Explain the most common form with **haben**. Examples in this chapter are: **hören, haben, kosten, lösen, öffnen, schmecken, wählen.** Ask students to work out the perfect tense of similar verbs from earlier chapters, for example: **wohnen, arbeiten, kaufen.**

The irregular and mixed verbs with **haben** which occur in this chapter are: **schlafen, essen, trinken, bringen.**

The separable verbs in this chapter are: anrufen, ausmachen, kennenlernen. Ask students to form the perfect tense of abholen and ausfüllen.

The verbs with sein in this chapter are: fahren, sein (ich war appears in the conversation on page 56, but only in the first person singular). Ask students to form the perfect tense of kommen and ankommen.

See page 69 of the coursebook for verbs beginning with be-, emp- etc. Those appearing in this chapter are: bestellen, reservieren, empfehlen. Ask students to give the perfect tense of: erwarten and studieren. Refer students to the list of irregular verbs on pages 138-9 of the coursebook.

Suggestion for further practice: Write up a list of past participles and ask students to choose an appropriate one to complete a brief story, for example: angekommen, erwartet, gegessen, geschlafen, gebracht.
    Wir haben ihn um 9 Uhr _____ aber er ist um 10 Uhr _____. Er hat gestern abend zu viel _____ und hat nicht gut _____. Ich habe ihm eine Tasse Kaffee _____ etc.

Subordinate clauses

An example of a subordinate clause appears in the recorded text on page 56: Wir können Ihnen später die Sehenswürdigkeiten der Stadt zeigen, wenn Sie Lust haben.

See section 3 on page 69. Give some examples then ask students to link sentences, for example:
    Wir müssen ihn anrufen. Er kommt nicht heute (wenn)
    Ich habe Schnitzel bestellt. Es schmeckt mir immer gut (weil)
    Wir haben in London gewohnt. Ich war ein kleines Kind (als).

Kapitel 6

Einkaufen

Main vocabulary	Asking for directions Buying souvenirs
Language	Verbs: **wissen, werden** (in the sense of 'to become'), **gefallen, passen** **Welche** Demonstrative pronouns

Directions

Include: rechts/links/geradeaus, bis zur/zum, entlang, hinunter, auf der rechten/linken Seite, die erste/zweite Straße.

Copy a street plan of your town or a German town or draw a basic town plan. Mark a couple of landmarks (church, park etc.) and designate the spot where you are starting from.

Explain slowly in German how to get there. When students seem to have grasped the vocabulary, mark a few more points on the plan and ask them to direct you or another student there.

Wissen

Write up **wissen** or refer to page 84 of the coursebook. Make sure students can distinguish between **wissen** and **kennen** (see Aufgabe 7).

Werden

Make sure students can distinguish between **werden** and **bekommen** (see Aufgabe 10).

Welche

Write up **welche** or refer to page 85 of the coursebook. Ask students to supply the correct part of **welche** (see also Aufgabe 3).

_____ Hotel empfehlen Sie?
_____ Flasche möchten Sie?
In _____ Gasthof arbeitet er? etc.

Demonstrative pronouns

Refer to page 84 of the coursebook. Ask students to try some of the following:
  a) Sie brauchen einen Schlüssel?
     ____ bekommen Sie am Empfang.
  b) Sie suchen eine Speisekarte?
     ____ bekommen Sie vom Kellner.
  c) Sie brauchen eine Fahrkarte?
     ____ bekommen Sie von dem Automaten.
  d) Sie wollen ein Geschenk kaufen?
     ____ bekommen Sie im ersten Stock.

(See also Aufgabe 11.)

Kapitel 7

Krankheit und Unfall

Main vocabulary	Common ailments At the doctor's/chemist's
Language	**Seit wann?** **Wie lange schon?** Modal verbs Imperative of separable verbs

Health

Suggestion: Make a large basic drawing of a thoroughly miserable specimen. He can then be labelled with all the ailments listed in the chapter. See pages 88–9. Naturally the poor chap will need to see a doctor.

Introduce: **Termin, Sprechstunden/Sprechstundenhilfe, Krankenschein, Rezept.**

After listening to the first cassette conversation, there is plenty of opportunity for practice in exercises 2 and 3 on pages 87–8 before John Faulkner sets off for the **Apotheke**.

Introduce: **einnehmen, bis sie alle aufgebraucht sind, nachlassen** before listening to the second cassette conversation.

Seit/schon

Suggestion: Make a few basic drawings of people. In one corner put a figure (40 Minuten, 1 Stunde etc.). You, or another student, ask(s):
Wie lange sind Sie schon da? to elicit: **Ich bin seit 40 Minuten/einer Stunde da.** etc.

Make a list of information about someone, for example:

Herr Braun:	verheiratet	– 1970
	Firma Breuer	– 1975
	Schwimmbad im Garten	– 1981
	Ferienhaus in Spanien	– 1986 etc.

Students ask: **Wie lange ist er schon verheiratet?** or **Seit wann ist er verheiratet?** to elicit: **Er ist seit _____ Jahren verheiratet** etc.

Modal verbs

To practise modal verbs you can use 'rolling sentences'. Make up a basic sentence. Each student repeats the sentence in turn but changes or adds something on your instruction as follows:

Basic sentence:	**Wir müssen nach Bonn fahren.**
Add morgen:	**Wir müssen morgen nach . . .**
Change to sollen:	**Wir sollen morgen . . .**
Change to er:	**Er soll morgen . . .** etc.

The basic sentence can of course be more complex and more topical, for example:
Er muß die Tabletten dreimal täglich einnehmen.
Er soll seine Arbeitsunfähigkeitsbescheinigung vom Arzt abholen.

Kapitel 8

Geld, Bank und Post

Main vocabulary	Changing money at the bank Buying stamps at the post office
Language	**Einige/etwas** **Etwas/nichts** **Kein**

Auf der Bank

Use German and English money (or drawings) to demonstrate changing notes for coins. Introduce: **Schein, Münze, Stück, wechseln.** Write up the current exchange rate.

Explain:
Auf eine Geschäftsreise nach Deutschland oder auf Urlaub nehme ich Reiseschecks mit. Die bekomme ich von der Bank. Ich muß sie unterschreiben. (Try asking: **Warum muß ich sie unterschreiben?**)

Introduce: **Wechselkurs, Bargeld, Reiseschecks einlösen** before listening to the first cassette conversation. There is a lot of scope for practice on pages 99–101 of the coursebook

Auf dem Postamt

Set the scene using small cards with basic drawings of a parcel, letters, stamps or real props if possible. Introduce: **Paket, Brief(e), Briefmarken, Einwurf, Einlieferungsschein, wiegen, einwerfen.**

Listen to the cassette conversation. There is again a lot of scope for practice on pages 103–5 of the coursebook.

Einige/etwas

Give examples to show how **einige** and **etwas** are used, for example: **einige Banken, in einigen Hotels, einige Reiseschecks, etwas Geld, etwas Milch/Zucker/Wasser.**

Etwas/nichts

Give examples to show how **etwas** and **nichts** are used, for example: **etwas für die Kinder, etwas Neues, etwas Kleines, nichts Interessantes, nichts Besonderes.** (See also Aufgaben 2 and 8.)

Kein

Explain the singular and plural endings (notes on pages 39 and 107 of the coursebook should help with the singular and the plural respectively). Write up or make cards to help practise **kein** as follows:

Das Zimmer hat: Bad √   Dusche ×   Balkon ×   Telefon √
Das Hotel hat: Doppelzimmer √   Einzelzimmer √   Familienzimmer ×
Die Stadt hat: Bahnhof √   Flughafen ×   Schule √   Universität ×
Herr Schmidt hat: Schlüssel √   Gepäck √   Reservierung ×
Er möchte: Frühstück √   Mittagessen ×   Abendessen √
Er spricht: Deutsch √   Englisch ×   Italienisch ×
Der Gasthof hat: Garten √   Schwimmbad ×   Fahrstuhl ×

Describe the first example: **Das Zimmer hat keine Dusche und keinen Balkon** etc.

Kapitel 9

Auto und Zoll

Main vocabulary	Customs and car travel Buying petrol
Language	The comparative Word order with subordinate clauses Interrogatives

Interrogatives: Wohin? Wo?

Ask if students can explain the difference between wo and wohin.

   Wo ist er?   **Wohin fährt er?**

Wo bleibt er?   Wohin gehen Sie?
Wo kann ich Reiseschecks einlösen?   Wohin fliegt er?

(See Aufgabe 1.)

An der Zollgrenze

Explain: grüne Versicherungskarte, verzollen, durchsuchen, Stichprobe (die Beamten können nicht alle Fahrzeuge durchsuchen . . .).

When students know this vocabulary they should be able to follow the first cassette conversation.

An der Tankstelle

A basic drawing or diagram of a car would help to introduce the vocabulary relating to the conversation on page 112 and exercise 2 on page 113.

The comparative

Exercise 4 on page 113 gives plenty of opportunity to practise the comparative of schnell, teuer, billig, breit, lang etc. (See Aufgaben 3 and 4.)

Students could perhaps also compare staying in a youth hostel and a big hotel, or life in Limbach (page 80 in the coursebook) and life in Bonn (page 20).

Subordinate clauses and word order

This is best explained by giving examples; students could try the following sentences if you do the first one for them.
a) Ich bin noch müde, obwohl ich gut geschlafen habe.
b) Ich kann die Reiseschecks einlösen, wenn ich zur Bank gehe.
c) Ich muß ihn morgen sehen, weil er heute krank ist.
d) Er soll zum Arzt gehen, wenn er Schmerzen hat.

Examples of subordinate clauses appear in the coursebook on page 119. (See also Aufgabe 6.)

Kapitel 10

Stadtbesichtigung und Freizeit

| **Main vocabulary** | Sightseeing |
| | Expressing opinions |

Language	The imperfect tense
	Reflexive verbs
	The superlative
	Dependent infinitive clauses
	Towns/cities used as adjectives

The superlative

Schön, groß, elegant, bekannt occur in the text in the superlative form.

Give some examples using these adjectives and explain that adjective endings follow the normal pattern, for example: **der größte Park, die bekanntesten Straßen** etc.

Ask students to attempt some phrases such as: the most expensive hotels, the most famous building, the most interesting book, the lowest price. It would also be useful to teach irregular forms such as **best-/meist-**.

Reflexive verbs

Students already know **Es freut mich**. Write the format for reflexive verbs on the board or refer students to section 2 on page 130. Students could ask each other what their interests are.

Refer to the list of reflexive verbs on page 124. Ask students to work out how to say:
He is bored.
Sit down!
We can relax at home.
He fell in love with her.
They are looking forward to their holiday.

For further practice ask students about their hobbies and their most recent holiday. (See also Aufgabe 3.) The first cassette conversation could be played at this point.

Imperfect tense

War, hatten and **mußten** occur in the second cassette conversation, **begann** and **kamen** in the reading comprehension.

Write out the imperfect tense on the board or refer students to page 129 of the coursebook. Ask them to work out the imperfect tense of **sagen, machen, antworten** and **zeigen**.

Explain the different pattern for irregular verbs using **sein** as an example. Students may be comforted by the list of irregular verbs on pages 138-9 of the coursebook. (See also Aufgabe 5.)

Dependent clauses

An example appears on page 122 of the coursebook: **Wir freuen uns, Sie an Bord *zu* haben**. Give a few examples, for example:
Er versucht das Auto zu reparieren.
Es freut mich Sie kennenzulernen.

Ask students to say:
I am trying to telephone him.
They are helping him to write a letter.
I recommend (to) you to see this film.

(See also Aufgabe 4.)

There is no role-play section in Chapter 10. Instead there is a long list of questions which students should be able to ask and answer.

Many of the questions are easy and have been covered by the situations and vocabulary in the coursebook. Some are intended to encourage sustained speaking and students will need help with vocabulary. Questions such as those asking students to describe their work or a journey could be answered orally at first then in writing.

Aufgaben

Kapitel 1

Besuch aus Deutschland

Aufgabe 1

Complete the blanks with the correct form of the verb in brackets.

a) Ich (wohnen) _____ in Neuß.

b) Er (heißen) _____ Ewald Weidmann.

c) Es (freuen) _____ mich.

d) Ich (sein) _____ Student.

e) Er (haben) _____ eine Tochter.

f) Frau Schmidt (arbeiten) _____ als Sekretärin.

g) Wir (kommen) _____ aus Krefeld.

h) Mr Newby (erwarten) _____ Sie.

i) Sie (sprechen) _____ Deutsch.

j) Sie (sein) _____ Verkaufsleiter.

Aufgabe 2

Fill in the missing words.

a) Ich komme _____ England.

b) Ich arbeite _____ der Firma Edelmetall.

c) _____ freut mich, Sie kennenzulernen.

d) Sind Sie _____ ersten Mal hier?

e) Ich wünsche _____ einen _____ Aufenthalt.

Aufgabe 3

Fill in the blanks with **wo, was, woher** or **wie**.

a) _____ heißen *Sie?*

b) _____ kommen Sie?

c) _____ sind Sie von Beruf?

d) _____ wohnen Sie?

e) _____ buchstabieren Sie Ihren Namen?

Aufgabe 4

Check the recorded conversation on page 4 of the coursebook and find the word or phrase which means:

a) At home. _____

b) Often. _____

c) That's right. _____

d) Isn't it? _____

e) Perhaps. _____

f) Myself. _____

g) Excuse me. _____

Aufgabe 5

a) Ist Helmut Kohl Engländer?

Nein, er _____.

b) Ist Brigitte Bardot Amerikanerin?

Nein, sie _____.

c) Ist George Bush Franzose?

Nein, er _____.

d) Ist Kylie Minogue Kanadierin?

Nein, sie _____.

e) Sind Sie Deutsche(r)?

Nein, ich _____.

Aufgabe 6

a) Was ist sie von Beruf? _____

_____

b) Was ist er von Beruf? _____

_____

c) Was ist sie von Beruf? _____

_____

was ist sie?

d) Was ist er von Beruf? _____

_____

Aufgabe 7

Change the following statements into questions.

a) Er kommt aus England.

_____

b) Sie arbeitet bei der Firma Nordchemikalien.

_____

c) Sie wohnen in Dortmund.

_____

d) Er hat eine Tochter.

_____

Aufgabe 8

Ask these questions in a different way.

a) Ist er zum ersten Mal hier?

_____

b) Sind Sie Programmierer?

_____

c) Heißen Sie Müller?

_____

d) Sind Sie verheiratet?

_____

Aufgabe 9

Find another way to say:

a) Ich heiße . . .

_____

b) Er ist unverheiratet.

_____

c) Er kommt aus Deutschland.

_____

d) Sie kommt aus Kanada.

_____

Aufgabe 10

Use the text in Chapter 1 to correct the following statements.

a) Ewald Weidmann ist Amerikaner.

_____

b) Mr Newby arbeitet bei Sasshofer AG.

_____

c) Lotte Meyer kommt aus Frankfurt.

_____

d) Herr Weidmann wohnt in Bonn.

_____

e) Frau Williams ist Verkaufsleiterin.

_____

f) Herr Weidmann ist zum ersten Mal in England.

_____

Aufgabe 11

Fill in the missing words.

Ich _____ Marlies Saalbach. Ich studiere in Marburg. Ich bin _____ aber ich arbeite auch

_____ Sekretärin. Meine Mutter und mein Vater sind auch in Marburg. Ich wohne also _____

Hause.

Mein _____ ist Hans Nieß. Ich komme _____ Bonn. Ich bin verheiratet und habe _____

Tochter. Ich _____ Vertreter bei _____ Firma Schmidt Möbel. Ich lerne Englisch und komme

oft _____ England.

Kapitel 2

Wann fahren Sie?

Aufgabe 1

Put the verb in brackets in the right place.

a) Er möchte (kommen) nach England

b) Sie möchte (lernen) Englisch

c) Wir möchten (fliegen) nach Deutschland

d) Sie möchten (wohnen) in Bonn

Aufgabe 2

Arrange the following words to make a question.

a) bleiben/ich/soll/drei oder vier/Tage

b) er/kommen/soll/Düsseldorf/nach

c) Firma/wir/besuchen/die/sollen

d) Bahn/der/mit/wir/fahren/sollen

Aufgabe 3

Fill in the blanks with the missing part of the verb.

a) Ich hole Sie vom Bahnhof _____ .

b) Er kommt am Flughafen _____ .

c) Er _____ mit der Bahn weiter.

d) Sie _____ Herrn Newby vom Bahnhof ab.

e) Er fliegt von Manchester _____ .

Aufgabe 4

a) Wann ist Weihnachten?

_____

b) Wann ist Silvester?

_____

c) Wann ist Neujahr?

_____

d) Wann ist der Tag der Arbeit?

_____

e) Wann ist Allerheiligen?

_____

Aufgabe 5

Fill in the blanks with **ein, eine** or **einen**.

a) Herr Jung hat _____ Tochter.

b) Frau Schmidt hat _____ Sohn.

c) Frau Pölking hat _____ Kind.

d) _____ Geschäftsführer arbeitet oft am Samstag.

e) Nordchemikalien ist _____ Firma in Hamburg.

Aufgabe 6

Fill in the blanks with **der, die, das** or **den**.

a) _____ Zimmer ist für _____ Geschäftsführer.

b) _____ Produktionsleiter kommt am Freitag.

c) _____ Exportleiterin erwartet Sie.

d) _____ Hotel ist in Bonn.

e) _____ Sekretärin ruft _____ Produktionsleiter an.

Aufgabe 7

Fill in the blanks with **dem** or **der** or replace the preposition with the contracted form of the preposition and article.

a) Sie kommt aus _____ Schweiz.

b) Wir fahren mit _____ Zug.

c) Er fährt mit _____ Bahn.

d) Herr Bauer fährt zu _____ Messe.

e) Ich arbeite bei _____ Firma Sasshofer AG.

f) Ich hole Sie von _____ Bahnhof ab.

Aufgabe 8

Fill in the blanks with **einem** or **einer**.

a) Er kommt aus _____ Stadt in der Schweiz.

b) Sie arbeitet bei _____ Firma in Bonn.

c) Wir übernachten in _____ Hotel in Köln.

d) Er fährt zu _____ Messe in England.

Aufgabe 9

Answer the following questions giving the time in full.

a) Wann kommt sie?   (9.00)

_____

b) Wann fährt er?   (8.15)

_____

c) Wann holen Sie Frau Jung ab?   (10.45)

_____

d) Um wieviel Uhr erwarten Sie Mr Smith?   (11.30)

_____

e) Wann fährt der Zug? (12.20)

_____

Aufgabe 10

Change each sentence so that it starts with the word(s) in brackets.

a) Er fliegt nach England.   (Bald)

_____

b) Ich besuche die Firma Sasshofer.   (Am fünften Mai)

_____

c) Wir fahren nach Düsseldorf.   (Im Juli)

_____

d) Der Zug kommt in Köln an.   (Um 7 Uhr)

_____

e) Er fährt zur Messe.   (Am Freitag)

_____

Aufgabe 11

Look at the recorded conversation on pages 14–15 again and find the word or phrase which means:

a) Just a moment.   _____

b) Is that OK?   _____

c) That's right.   _____

d) You're welcome.   _____

Aufgabe 12

Fill in the missing word.

a) Er kommt bald ____ Besuch.

b) Er fährt ____ vierten Oktober.

c) Er fliegt ____ Manchester ab.

d) Er kommt ____ zehn Uhr an.

e) Wir fahren ____ der Bahn weiter.

Aufgabe 13

Complete the following sentences using the correct form of the possessive adjective.

a) Das Rathaus ist gegenüber (our) _____ Hotel.

b) Das is für (my) _____ Mutter.

c) Wie geht es (your) _____ Mann?

d) (His) _____ Frau heißt Anna.

e) Sie wohnt bei (her) _____ Mutter.

f) (Their) _____ Geschäftsführer kommt zu Besuch.

Aufgabe 14

Rewrite the following sentences using the future tense.

a) Ich spreche mit Frau Steiner.

_____

b) Ich lerne Deutsch.

_____

c) Sie reserviert ein Zimmer für den Direktor.

_____

d) Er fliegt nach München.

_____

Kapitel 3

Unterwegs

Aufgabe 1

Wann fährt der Zug? Answer giving the time in full.

a) 13.20

_____

b) 14.35

_____

c) 19.55

_____

d) 21.13

_____

Aufgabe 2

Fill in the blanks with **was, wo, wann, woher** or **wie**.

a) _____ geht es Ihnen?

b) _____ kostet das?

c) _____ fährt die S-Bahn ab?

d) _____ kommen Sie?

e) _____ komme ich in Düsseldorf an?

Aufgabe 3

Fill in the blanks with the correct form of **müssen**.

a) Ich _____ in Köln umsteigen.

b) Wir _____ den Automaten benutzen.

c) Er _____ nach Berlin fahren.

d) Sie _____ eine Fahrkarte kaufen.

Aufgabe 4

Change the following sentences into questions using the correct form of **können**.

a) Ich fahre direkt nach Berlin.

_____

b) Sie kommen am Montag.

_____

c) Wir kaufen die Fahrkarten im Zug.

_____

Aufgabe 5

Look at the recorded conversations on pages 28 and 30. Find the word or phrase which means:

a) Over there.   _____

b) Escalator.   _____

c) Return.   _____

d) Only.   _____

Aufgabe 6

Complete the following sentences using the correct form of the personal pronoun.

a) (I) _____ hole (him) _____ vom Bahnhof ab.

b) (He) _____ erwartet (her) _____ um neun Uhr.

c) (You) _____ bleiben eine Woche bei (us) _____.

d) (We) _____ erwarten (them) _____ am Freitag.

e) (She) _____ wird ein Zimmer für (me) _____ reservieren.

f) (They) _____ danken (me).

g) (He) _____ kann (her) _____ helfen.

h) (She) _____ gibt (you) _____ die Fahrkarte.

Aufgabe 7

Look at the reading comprehension on page 37 again. Find the word or phrase which means:

a) Capital city. _____

b) Neighbouring countries. _____

c) Trade. _____

d) For example. _____

e) Mainly. _____

Aufgabe 8

Give the questions to which the following sentences are the answers.

a) _____
   Der Zug nach Hannover fährt um 14.25.

b) _____
   Von Gleis drei.

c) _____
   Nein, Sie müssen in Köln umsteigen.

d) _____
   Einfach bitte.

e) _____
   Zweiter Klasse bitte.

Aufgabe 9

Complete the following sentences using the correct form of the definite article.

a) Der Fahrpreis erscheint oberhalb _____ Tastenreihe.

b) Er kommt während _____ Woche.

c) Sie wohnen außerhalb _____ Stadt.

d) Während _____ Aufenthalts besucht er die Firma.

Aufgabe 10

Fill in the missing words.

Ich möchte mit _____ Zug _____ Berlin fahren. _____ nächste Zug fährt _____ 13.20.

Ich kann aber nicht _____ fahren. Ich muß in Hannover _____.

Ich will zweiter _____ fahren. Einfach kostet die _____ DM 102. Hin und _____ kostet sie

DM 204. Ich will in zwei Tagen zurückkommen, ich zahle also DM _____.

Aufgabe 11

Change the following into sentences using the correct form of **wollen**.

a) Ich kaufe eine Fahrkarte.

_____

b) Wir wechseln einen Fünfhundertmarkschein.

_____

c) Er fährt mit dem Zug um 11.30.

_____

d) Sie benutzen den Automaten.

_____

e) Frau Schmidt fährt direkt nach Hamburg.

_____

Aufgabe 12

Complete the following sentences using the correct form of the word in brackets.

a) Ich danke (you) _____ für die Auskunft.

b) Wir empfehlen (you) _____ das Hotel Anker.

c) Der Beamte hilft (me) _____ am Bahnhof.

d) Wir danken (them) _____ für ihre Hilfe.

Kapitel 4

Unterkunft in Deutschland

Aufgabe 1

Use the following vocabulary to give commands.

a) Anmeldeformular/ausfüllen

b) Zimmer/für den Geschäftsführer/reservieren

c) mein Gepäck/nach oben/bringen

d) mich/vom Bahnhof/abholen

Aufgabe 2

Fill in the gaps with the correct form of the comparative adjective.

a)

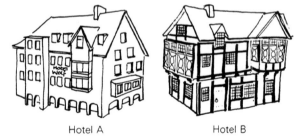

Hotel A   Hotel B

Hotel A ist alt, aber Hotel B ist _____.

b)

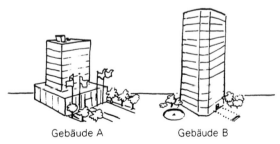

Gebäude A   Gebäude B

Gebäude A is groß, aber Gebäude B ist

_____.

c)

Buch A   Buch B

Buch A ist billig, aber Buch B ist _____.

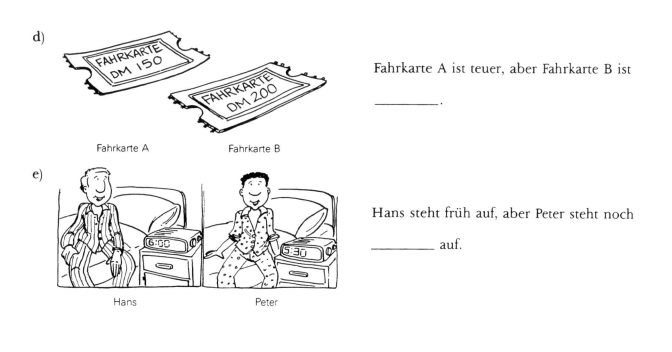

d) **Fahrkarte A** **Fahrkarte B**

Fahrkarte A ist teuer, aber Fahrkarte B ist

_____ .

e) **Hans** **Peter**

Hans steht früh auf, aber Peter steht noch

_____ auf.

Aufgabe 3

Look at the information about the three hotels on page 48 again and correct the following statements.

a) Das Hotel Restaurant Adler hat 50 Betten.

_____

b) Im Hotel Central kostet eine Übernachtung mit Frühstück DM 95.

_____

c) Das Hotel Central hat keinen Ruhetag.

_____

d) Der Gasthof Krone hat seine eigene Bäckerei.

_____

e) Im Hotel Adler gibt es den ganzen Tag warme Küche.

_____

Aufgabe 4

Fill in the blanks.

a) Der Gasthof ist gut, aber das Hotel ist _____ .

b) Ich trinke gern Bier, aber ich trinke _____ Wein.

c) Wir lernen viel zu Hause, aber wir lernen _____ in der Schule.

d) Im Winter ist der Schwarzwald schön, aber im Sommer ist er noch _____ .

Aufgabe 5

Replace the noun with the correct pronoun.

a) Wo ist der Fahrstuhl?   _____ ist um die Ecke.

b) Wo ist das Gepäck?   _____ ist im Auto.

c) Wo ist die Fahrkarte?   _____ ist in meiner Tasche.

d) Hast du den Schlüssel?   Ja, ich habe _____.

e) Kennen Sie Frau Pölking?   Ja, ich kenne _____.

f) Nehmen Sie das Zimmer?   Ja, ich nehme _____.

Aufgabe 6

Look at the reading comprehension on page 51 and find the word or phrase which means:

a) Suitable accommodation.   _____

b) Luxury hotels.   _____

c) Conference rooms.   _____

d) Businessmen.   _____

e) Prices per night.   _____

f) For every taste.   _____

Aufgabe 7

a)

Das alt__ Büro

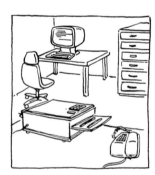
Ein modern__ Büro

b)

Die englisch__
Verkaufsleiterin

Eine jung__ Sekretärin

Der neu__
Geschäftsführer

Eine wichtig__ Kundin

d)

Wo arbeitet die jung__ Sekretärin?
Sie arbeitet in d__ alt__ Büro.

e)

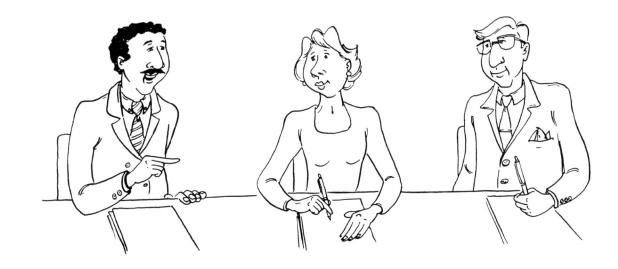

Wo sitzt der wichtig__ Kunde?
Er sitzt neben d__ englisch__ Verkaufsleiterin.

Wo sitzt die englisch__ Verkaufsleiterin?
Sie sitzt zwischen d__ wichtigen Kunde__ und d__ neu__ Geschäftsführer.

Aufgabe 8

a)

Ein klein__ Gasthof

b)

Ein erstklassig__ Hotel

c)

Ein__ modern__
Jugendherberge

d)

Wo wohnt er? Er wohnt
in ein__ klein__
Gasthof.

e)

Wo wohnt er? Er wohnt
in ein__ teuer__
Hotel.

f)

Wo wohnt er? Er wohnt
in ein__ modern__
Jugendherberge.

g)

Ich suche ein__ klein__
Gasthof.

h)

Ich suche ein
erstklassig__ Hotel für
unsere Konferenz.

i)

Ich suche ein__
modern__
Jugendherberge.

Aufgabe 9

Write a letter in German to Herrn Jeismann of Maschinenfabrik Schmidt GmbH confirming his visit to your company. Include the following information.

He is due to arrive in England on September 14th and stay until 19th. You are expecting him on 17–18th. Recommend a hotel and say you will provisionally book a room there for the relevant dates. Tell him you will soon be sending more information about your prices and sales conditions.

Aufgabe 10

Fill in the correct adjective endings.

Herr Schmidt ist Chef ein__ klein__ Firma in Düsseldorf.

Sein__ Firma sucht neu__ Kunden in England.

Heute ist im Büro ein__ gut__ Geschäftsfreund__.

Dies__ Freund hat eine interessant__ Information für ihn.

Wegen dies__ neu__ Information kann Herr Schmidt jetzt ein__ kurz__

Besuch nach England planen.

Aufgabe 11

Mr and Mrs Brown are on holiday in Germany. They do not know the language very well. Speak to the receptionist for them.

They want a double room for two nights. They are going sightseeing during the day so would like half board. They would prefer a room with a shower and need to know when the meals are served.

Empfang: Guten Tag!

Sie: _____

Empfang: Für wieviele Nächte?

Sie: _____

Empfang: Möchten Sie Vollpension?

Sie: _____

Empfang: Möchten Sie ein Zimmer mit Bad oder mit Dusche?

Sie: _____

Empfang: Von 7.00 bis 9.15 Uhr.

Sie: _____

Empfang: Von 18.00 bis 21.30 Uhr.

Sie: Vielen Dank.

Kapitel 5

Essen und Trinken

Aufgabe 1

Your German guest arrived in England last night. Use the prompts to ask him polite questions.

a) Sie/gut/schlafen?

_____

b) gute Reise/haben?

_____

c) viel/von unserer Stadt/hören?

_____

d) unseren Verkaufsleiter/schon/kennenlernen?

_____

Aufgabe 2

Complete the following sentences using the correct form of the pronoun.

a) Sauerkraut schmeckt (me) _____ nicht.

b) Es geht (him) _____ besser.

c) Schmeckt es (you) _____?

d) Wie geht es (her) _____?

e) Ich empfehle (you) _____ das Hotel Coenen.

Aufgabe 3

Fill in the gaps with the past participle of the verb in brackets.

a) Er hat ein Zimmer (reservieren) _____.

b) Als Nachtisch habe ich Eis (bekommen) _____.

c) Er hat mir das Hotel (empfehlen) _____.

d) Mein Kollege hat Schnitzel (bestellen) _____.

e) Wir haben die Firma (besuchen) _____.

f) Wir haben ihn um 9 Uhr (erwarten) _____.

Aufgabe 4

Look at the reading comprehension on page 66 and find the word or phrase which means:

a) A boiled egg. _____

b) Main meal. _____

c) Either . . . or. _____

d) Consists of. _____

e) Expression. _____

Aufgabe 5

Fill in the gaps with the past participle of the verb in brackets.

Ich habe ihn heute morgen (anrufen) _____, aber er war nicht da. Er ist schon um 7 Uhr

(abfahren) _____. Er ist um 8.20 Uhr von Düsseldorf (abfliegen) _____. Er hat mich später

(anrufen) _____. Er ist um 9 Uhr in London (ankommen) _____. Wir haben ihn vom Flughafen

(abholen) _____.

Aufgabe 6

Join the following sentences with weil.

a) Er will jetzt essen. Er hat Hunger.

_____

b) Er kann kein Zimmer bekommen. Er hat keine Reservierung.

_____

c) Ich kann ihm nicht schreiben. Ich kenne seine Adresse nicht.

_____

d) Darf ich die Rechnung haben? Ich muß gleich gehen.

_____

e) Ich möchte gern die Stadt sehen. Ich habe so viel davon gehört.

_____

f) Er ist nicht mehr müde. Er hat gut geschlafen.

_____

Aufgabe 7

Rewrite the following sentences so that they start with **gestern**.

a) Er fährt um elf Uhr ab.

_____

b) Ich fahre mit der Bahn.

_____

c) Er kommt nicht zum Mittagessen.

_____

d) Wir kommen um 18.00 Uhr an.

_____

e) Sie fliegt von London ab.

_____

f) Wir steigen in Köln um.

_____

Aufgabe 8

Expand the following phrases to full sentences to make an entry in your German diary.

Gestern Abend – Hotel zum Adler – 7.30 ankommen – 8 Uhr essen – Vorspeise Ochsenschwanzsuppe wählen – Hauptgericht Wiener Schnitzel – Flasche Rheinwein trinken – keinen Nachtisch bestellen – ziemlich viel kosten – weil ein gutes Hotel

Gestern Abend war ich im Hotel zum Adler . . .

Aufgabe 9

Join the following sentences with **obwohl**.

a) Ich esse gern im Hotel zum Adler. Das Essen ist ziemlich teuer.

_____

b) Ich kenne die Sehenswürdigkeiten der Stadt nicht. Ich bin schon zweimal hier gewesen.

_____

c) Wir sind nach München geflogen. Ich fliege nicht gern.

_____

d) Er hat um 4 Uhr ein Stück Kuchen gegessen. Er hat erst um 2 Uhr zu Mittag gegessen.

_____

Aufgabe 10

Look at the conversation **im Restaurant** on pages 58-9 and correct the following statements.

a) Der Kellner zeigt ihnen einen Tisch am Fenster.

_____

b) Herr Walter hat einen Tisch für drei Personen reserviert.

_____

c) Herr Newby bestellt Sauerbraten.

_____

d) Als Vorspeise ißt Frau Meyer einen kleinen Salat.

_____

e) Herr Newby ißt gern Zitroneneis.

_____

Aufgabe 11

Fill in the gaps with **gern** or **lieber**.

a) Ich esse _____ Sauerbraten, aber ich esse _____ Schnitzel.

b) Er trinkt sehr _____ Bier.

c) Möchten Sie eine Tasse Kaffee? _____ Tee bitte.

d) Möchten Sie die Stadt sehen? Ja, _____.

e) Möchten Sie die Ochsenschwanzsuppe? Ja, die esse ich sehr _____.

Kapitel 6

Einkaufen

Aufgabe 1

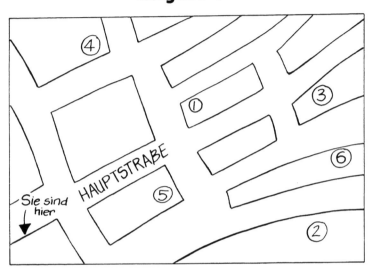

Key
1 Die Post
2 Der Park
3 Die Buchhandlung
4 die Bank
5 Die Parfümerie
6 der Verkehrsverein

Wie komme ich am besten

a) zum Park? _____

b) zum Verkehrsverein? _____ .___

c) zur Buchhandlung? _____

d) zur Parfümerie? _____

e) zur Post? _____

f) zur Bank? _____

Aufgabe 2

Fill in the blanks with the correct personal pronoun.

a) Gefällt (you) _____ das Kleid?

b) Es gefällt (me) _____ gut.

c) Die Hose paßt (him) _____ nicht.

d) Die Schuhe passen (her) _____ .

e) Hoffentlich gefällt (them) _____ das Geschenk.

41

Aufgabe 3

Fill in the blanks with the correct part of **welche**.

a) Ich möchte ein T-Shirt.

_____ Größe möchten Sie?

b) Ich suche ein Andenken.

In _____ Geschäft finde ich es?

c) Ich suche ein Restaurant.

_____ Restaurant empfehlen Sie?

d) Ich möchte Parfüm kaufen.

In _____ Stock ist die Parfümerie?

e) Ich will einen Koffer kaufen.

In _____ Abteilung finde ich die?

Aufgabe 4

Fill in the blanks with the correct form of the indefinite pronoun.

a) Diese Kassetten gefallen meiner Tochter bestimmt.

Ich nehme _____.

b) Die Bücher sind sehr preiswert.

Ich nehme _____.

c) Diese Filme sind sehr gut.

Ich nehme _____.

d) Diese Hemden passen meinem Sohn bestimmt.

Ich kaufe ihm _____.

Aufgabe 5

Look at the prices of foodstuffs on page 79 of the coursebook and find the words which mean:
a) Fish fingers. _____
b) Mince. _____
c) Pineapple. _____
d) Cod. _____
e) Cauliflower. _____

Aufgabe 6

Look at the advertisement on page 75 again and correct the following statements.
a) Bei Foto Goertz kann man Farbbilder innerhalb von 48 Stunden bekommen.

_____

b) Bei Mössing kauft man Parfüm.

_____

c) Beim Weinmann Tscharke gibt es über 500 Sorten Weine und Spirituosen.

_____

d) Die Stadtparfümerie Pieper hat nur ein Geschäft im Ruhrgebiet.

_____

e) Die Buchhandlung Grauert ist am Flughafen.

_____

Aufgabe 7

Fill in the gaps with the correct form of **kennen** or **wissen**.

a) Wo ist er? Ich _____ es nicht.

b) _____ Sie Herrn Jung?

c) Ja, wir _____ uns schon.

d) Frau Buch _____ nicht wann er kommt.

e) Frau Buch _____ Herrn Jung. Er kommt immer spät an.

Aufgabe 8

Fill in the blanks with **wo, was, welche(s), warum** or **was für**.

a) _____ Farbe möchten Sie?

b) _____ kostet die Kassette?

c) _____ gehen Sie zur Kö? In der Altstadt können Sie billiger einkaufen.

d) _____ kann man hier billig einkaufen?

e) _____ T-shirt gefällt Ihnen am besten?

f) _____ Spielzeuge suchen Sie?

Aufgabe 9

Answer the following questions using all the information in Chapter 6.

a) Heute ist der zweite Samstag des Monats. Kann ich um 15.00 Uhr einkaufen gehen?

_____

b) Wieviele Einwohner hat Limbach?

_____

c) Gibt es ein Theater in Limbach?

_____

d) Kann eine deutsche Familie normalerweise viel Geld im Monat sparen?

_____

e) Was muß man zuerst vom Bruttoeinkommen abziehen?

_____

Aufgabe 10

Fill in the gaps with the correct form of **werden** or **bekommen**.

a) Meine Tochter ist im Juli sechs _____.

b) Wir haben eine Tasse Kaffee _____.

c) Die Kinder _____ müde.

d) Im Winter _____ es schon um 16.00 Uhr dunkel.

e) Er _____ viel Geld im Monat.

f) Wir haben eine Postkarte von ihm _____.

Aufgabe 11

Fill in the gaps using the correct part of the demonstrative pronoun.

a) Wo kann ich Geschenke kaufen?

   _____ finden Sie im dritten Stock.

b) Ich nehme einen Rheinwein.

   _____ trinke ich sehr gern.

c) Ich kaufe ihr eine neue Uhr.

   _____ hier gefällt ihr bestimmt.

d) Ich möchte einen Film kaufen.

   _____ bekommen Sie bestimmt bei Foto Goertz.

Kapitel 7

Krankheit und Unfall

Aufgabe 1

Give commands.

Example: Mich abholen!
             Holen Sie mich ab.

a) Ihn anrufen!

_____

b) Mit der Bahn weiterfahren!

_____

c) In Köln umsteigen!

_____

d) Ihren Paß mitbringen!

_____

Aufgabe 2

Was fehlt ihm?

a) _____

b) _____

c) _____

d) _____

Aufgabe 3

Complete the conversation with the correct word from the following list:

Termin, Sprechstunde, Apotheke, Rezept, Schmerzen

Herr Jung: Wann haben Sie _____?

Stimme: Von 10–12 Uhr und von 15–17 Uhr.

Herr Jung: Ich möchte einen _____ für heute. Geht das?

Stimme: Ja, kommen Sie um 15.30.

Herr Jung: Ich habe Magenweh.

Arzt: Wie lange haben Sie schon diese _____?

Herr Jung: Seit zwei Tagen.

Arzt: Hmm. Ich gebe Ihnen ein _____. Bringen Sie es zur _____. Die finden Sie gegenüber der Bank.

Aufgabe 4

Look at the advertisements on page 91 again and find the word or phrase which means:

a) Speedy recovery. _____

b) To spray. _____

c) Cough drops. _____

d) Healthy sleep. _____

e) Works for hours. _____

Aufgabe 5

Ask how long something has been going on using **Wie lange schon . . . ?** or **Seit wann?**

Example: arbeiten – Firma Sasshofer?
Wie lange arbeiten Sie schon bei der Firma Sasshofer? or
Seit wann arbeiten Sie bei der Firma Sasshofer?

a) wohnen – Neuß?

_____

b) lernen – deutsch?

_____

c) sein – in Deutschland?

_____

d) studieren – in Bonn?

_____

Aufgabe 6

Use the information in Chapter 7 to help you answer these questions using **müssen**.

a) Warum muß John Faulkner seine Tabletten einnehmen?

_____

b) Was muß er machen, wenn die Schmerzen nicht nachlassen?

_____

c) Ihr Kollege ist die Treppe herunter gefallen. Sein Rücken tut sehr weh. Was müssen Sie machen?

_____

d) Ich bin seit zwei Tagen krank, und morgen kann ich auch noch nicht arbeiten. Was muß ich machen?

_____

Aufgabe 7

Look at the reading comprehension on page 93 and correct the following statements.

a) In Österreich wird die Einwohnerzahl jedes Jahr größer.

_____

b) Die maximale Entfernung von Norden nach Süden ist 560 Kilometer.

_____

c) Österreich ist in zehn Bundesländer eingeteilt.

_____

d) Der Bundesrat hat 165 Vertreter.

_____

e) Viele der österreichischen Arbeiter sind auf dem Land beschäftigt.

_____

Aufgabe 8

Fill in the gaps with the correct form of **müssen** or **dürfen**.

a) Meine Mutter hat heute Geburtstag.

   Ich _____ ihr ein Geschenk kaufen.

b) Ich habe Tabletten von der Apotheke bekommen.

   Ich _____ sie dreimal täglich einnehmen.

c) Dieses Hemd gefällt mir.

   Sie _____ es anprobieren, wenn Sie wollen.

d) Ich bin zum ersten Mal hier.

   Also _____ wir Ihnen die Sehenswürdigkeiten der Stadt zeigen?

Aufgabe 9

You are at work at your company's German branch. A colleague in the same office is taken ill. There is a doctor in the building. Phone him and give him the following information.

Herr Saalbach has had a sore throat and a cough since yesterday. Now he has a headache too and seems feverish. He has got some cough drops from the chemist's but they are not helping him. You think he ought to see the doctor soon.

Aufgabe 10

Look at the text on pages 89–90 of the coursebook and find the following phrases:

a) Until they are all used up.

_____

b) I can hardly breathe.

_____

c) Three tablets per day.

_____

d) If the pain does not ease.

_____

e) My nose is blocked.

_____

Kapitel 8

Geld, Bank und Post

Aufgabe 1

Look at the text on page 98 of the coursebook and answer the following questions.

a) Was müssen Sie dem Angestellten zeigen, wenn Sie Reiseschecks einlösen wollen?

_____

b) Was müssen Sie dann machen, bevor Sie das Geld bekommen?

_____

c) Wieviel Geld will der Exportleiter wechseln?

_____

d) Wieviele DM bekommt er für ein Pfund?

_____

e) Bekommt er das Geld direkt vom Angestellten?

_____

Aufgabe 2

Fill in the blanks with **einige** or **etwas**.

a) Er hat _____ Geld.

b) Ich habe _____ Kleingeld.

c) In _____ Hotels kann man auch Geld wechseln.

d) _____ Banken haben auch Geldautomaten.

Aufgabe 3

Look at the advertisement for the cash dispenser on page 101 of the coursebook. Find the word or phrase which means:

a) Increasingly. _____

b) Make use of. _____

c) Secret number. _____

d) Recognise. _____

49

Aufgabe 4

Look at the conversation on page 102 of the coursebook and then fill in the missing words.

a) Ich möchte zwei Briefmarken _____ einer Mark.

b) Sonst _____ etwas?

c) Ihr Paket _____ 750 Gramm.

d) Ins Inland oder ins _____?

e) Wo kann ich die Briefe einwerfen?

   Der _____ ist gegenüber _____ fünf.

Aufgabe 5

Write a letter or make a telephone call to complain about the following situation:

The parcel you sent to a friend has not arrived. It weighed 630 g. Postage cost DM 13.50. You have a certificate of posting. You posted it at 9.20 a.m. on the 15th, it is now the 22nd. It is most urgent that they find the parcel.

Aufgabe 6

Look at the reading comprehension on page 105 of the coursebook and correct the following statements.

a) Eine Million Menschen arbeiten für die Deutsche Bundespost.

   _____

b) Ein Viertel der Arbeiter sind Frauen.

   _____

c) Die Bundesdruckerei hat ihren Hauptsitz in Bonn.

   _____

d) Die Postleitzahl von Berlin ist 2000.

   _____

Aufgabe 7

Fill in the blanks with the correct form of kein.

a) Er hat _____ Geld.

b) Sie hat _____ Paß.

c) Sie haben _____ Kinder.

d) Er hat _____ Tabletten vom Arzt bekommen.

e) Ich darf _____ Alkohol trinken.

f) Wir haben _____ Paket bekommen.

Aufgabe 8

Fill in the gaps using **viel**, **etwas** or **nichts**.

a) Die Messe gefällt mir. Es gibt _____ Neues da.

b) Ich höre nicht sehr gut. Sie müssen _____ lauter sprechen.

c) Er hat ein sehr großes Haus gekauft. Er hat _____ Geld.

d) Diese Messe ist nicht gut, ich finde _____ Interessantes hier.

e) Gibt es _____ unter dem Tisch?

   Nein, es gibt _____ da.

Aufgabe 9

Fill in the gaps with **etwas** or **kein**.

a) Bringen Sie uns _____ Milch bitte!

   Es tut mir leid, wir haben _____ Milch.

b) Wir haben _____ Zeit. Der Zug fährt gleich ab.

c) Können Sie mir diesen Schein wechseln?

   Es tut mir leid, ich habe _____ Kleingeld.

d) Wir haben leider _____ Butter mehr.

Aufgabe 10

You are going on a business trip to Switzerland. Ask a colleague to order some currency for you. Use the following prompts to help:

Business trip – Basel
Travellers' cheques – DM 1000 (10 × DM 100 cheques)
Swiss currency – DM 250
Rate of exchange?
Do you need your passport?
You would like to collect them at 11.30 tomorrow morning.

Auto und Zoll

Aufgabe 1

Fill in the gaps with **wohin, wie, wieviel** or **wo**.

a) _____ fahren Sie?

b) _____ ist die Bank?

c) _____ weit ist das von hier?

d) _____ geht er jetzt?

e) _____ hat es gekostet?

f) _____ komme ich zum Parkplatz?

Aufgabe 2

Können Sie das auf Deutsch erklären?

a) Was ist eine grüne Versicherungskarte?

_____

b) Warum braucht man eine Versicherungskarte im Ausland?

_____

c) Was ist eine Stichprobe?

_____

d) Warum machen die Zollbeamten Stichproben?

_____

Aufgabe 3

Fill in the gaps with the correct form of the comparative.

a) Es dauert nicht (lang) _____ als 10 Minuten.

b) Der Wein hier ist (billig) _____ als im Hotel.

c) Die Geschäfte sind (teuer) _____ als in der Altstadt.

d) In der Bank ist der Kurs (gut) _____ als im Hotel.

e) Ein Auslandsbrief kostet (viel) _____ als ein Inlandsbrief.

Aufgabe 4

Change the sentences using the comparative.

Example: Brücke A ist 20 Meter hoch. Brücke B ist 15 Meter hoch. (niedrig)
Brücke B ist niedriger als Brücke A.

a) Die Merkurstr. ist 10 Meter breit. Die Alexanderstr. ist 8 Meter breit. (eng)

_____

b) Zürich hat 356,800 Einwohner. Basel hat 177, 900 Einwohner. (groß)

_____

c) In einer Pension kostet eine Übernachtung circa DM 40. In einem Hotel kostet eine Übernachtung circa DM 60. (teuer)

_____

d) Die T-Shirts hier kosten DM 20 und im Kaufhaus kosten sie DM 6.50. (billig)

_____

e) Anna ist 10 Jahre alt. Thomas ist 8 Jahre alt. (alt)

_____

Aufgabe 5

Look at the conversations on pages 109 and 112 in the coursebook and find the word or phrase which means:

a) I am delivering books. _____

b) How annoying! _____

c) How long will it take? _____

d) I only checked it the day before yesterday. _____

e) Check the tyre pressure please. _____

Aufgabe 6

Rewrite the following sentences so that they start with the subordinate clause.

Example: Sie müssen hier warten, wenn Sie etwas zu verzollen haben.
Wenn Sie etwas zu verzollen haben, . . .

a) Ich fahre gern meinen VW Polo, obwohl ein BMW schneller ist.

_____

b) Er muß bis 19.00 Uhr im Büro bleiben, weil er noch viel zu erledigen hat.

_____

c) Wir müssen viel Geld sparen, weil ich nach Australien fahren will.

_____

d) Ich habe ihn kennengelernt, als ich ein kleines Kind war.

_____

Aufgabe 7

Look at the reading comprehension on page 116 of the coursebook and correct the following statements.

a) Die Nachbarländer der Schweiz sind Deutschland, Österreich, Frankreich und Spanien.

_____

b) Es gibt sechs Flughäfen in der Schweiz.

_____

c) Die Hauptexporte sind Uhren und Lebensmittel.

_____

d) Basel ist größer als Zürich.

_____

e) Das Land ist in 62 Kantone eingeteilt.

_____

Aufgabe 8

Look at the at-sight translation on page 114 of the coursebook and find the word or phrase which means:

a) Minimum age. _____

b) Curriculum vitae. _____

c) Successful. _____

d) Photograph. _____

e) Certificate. _____

Aufgabe 9

Give the questions to which the following are the answers.

a) _____

Es dauert nur zehn Minuten.

b) _____

Nein, ich habe nur 2 Flaschen Wein und 50 Zigaretten.

c) _____

Ich bin heute ungefähr 200 Kilometer gefahren.

d) _____

Danke, ich habe den Reifendruck schon geprüft.

Aufgabe 10

Use all the information in Chapter 9 to answer the following questions.

a) Warum müssen die Zollbeamten einige Fahrzeuge durchsuchen?

_____

b) Welche Papiere braucht man, wenn man ins Ausland fahren will.

_____

c) Welches Auto fährt schneller, ein Opel Corsa oder ein VW Polo?

_____

d) Wenn man in England eine Panne hat, kann man den AA rufen. Wen ruft man in Deutschland?

_____

e) Wieviele Einwohner hat die Hauptstadt der Schweiz?

_____

Kapitel 10

Stadtbesichtigung und Freizeit

Aufgabe 1

Make everything superlative.

a) Es ist das (gut) _____ Restaurant in der Stadt.

b) Das ist das (teuer) _____ Geschäft in der Stadt.

c) Wir sind im (ruhig) _____ Hotel in der Stadt.

d) Wir haben das (bequem) _____ Zimmer im Hotel.

e) Er arbeitet bei der (neu) _____ Firma in der Stadt.

f) Es ist der (groß) _____ Flughafen Europas.

Aufgabe 2

Look at the information about the river trip on page 122 of the coursebook and find the word or phrase which means:

a) An experience. _____

b) A pleasure. _____

c) To miss. _____

d) On no account. _____

e) Excursions. _____

Aufgabe 3

You met Herr Jung last year in Germany. Now he is visiting you. Complete the gaps with an appropriate reflexive verb.

Sie:　　　　Bitte _____ Sie _____! Es _____ _____ sehr, Sie wiederzusehen.

Herr Jung: Danke, gleichfalls. Ich habe _____ sehr _____ diesen Besuch _____.

Sie:　　　　Wir wollen Ihnen die Sehenswürdigkeiten der Stadt zeigen. _____ Sie _____ für eine Stadtbesichtigung?

Herr Jung: Ja, gerne.

Sie: Haben Sie noch einen Wunsch? Wir wollen, daß Sie _____ bei uns _____. Wie ist Ihr Hotel?

Herr Jung: Ausgezeichnet danke! Es _____ _____ neben dem Park, aber es ist auch nicht weit

von der Stadtmitte. Ich habe es _____ dort ganz _____ _____.

Aufgabe 4

Put the second half of the sentence into German. You will need to use **zu**.

Example: Wir freuen uns, (to have you as a guest)
Wir freuen uns, Sie als Gast zu haben.

a) Es freut mich, (to see you again)

_____

b) Ich empfehle Ihnen, (to do a tour of the city)

_____

c) Er hilft mir, (to learn German)

_____

d) Wir hoffen es sehr, (to see you next year in Germany)

_____

e) Wir versuchen, (to offer you an interesting programme)

_____

Aufgabe 5

A businesswoman is talking about someone she has not seen for a long time. Choose verbs from the list to complete her story.

kam, erkannte, hatte, studierte, interessierte, erinnerte, arbeitete, saß

Er _____ auf der Universität in Bonn und _____ nie Zeit sich zu entspannen. Damals _____

er sich nur für sein Studium. Später _____ er bei einer Firma in Düsseldorf. Er _____ gestern

am nächsten Tisch im Restaurant aber ich _____ ihn nicht. Später, als ich nach Hause _____,

_____ ich mich an seinen Namen.

Aufgabe 6

Give the German for:

a) An English newspaper. _____

b) Frankfurt trade fair. _____

c) The Munich Beer Festival. _____

d) In a London bus. _____

e) A German company. _____

f) In Düsseldorf airport. _____

Aufgabe 7

Look at the reading comprehension on page 127 of the coursebook and find the word or phrase which means:

a) Sword. _____

b) Cutting implements. _____

c) Just under half an hour. _____

d) People who work at home. _____

e) In their own workshops. _____

Aufgabe 8

You are going to a trade fair in Munich for three days. Your hosts are trying to arrange sightseeing and other entertainment for you. Write and tell them what you are keen to see. Use the prompts if you want!

Freue mich – Besuch – erstes Mal in Deutschland – obwohl Messe – wichtigster Teil – auch gern Stadt sehen. Interessiere mich für Musik, Theater, Museen, Bier . . . Viel von der Stadt gehört – die Gegend sehr schön. Hoffentlich keinen Dolmetscher brauchen! Bedanke mich . . .

Aufgabe 9

Complete the questions to which the following are the answers.

a) _____ in der Welt?
   Everest

b) _____ in England?
   Scafell Pike

c) _____ in der Welt?
   Der Nil

d) _____ in England?
   Der Severn

e) _____ in Paris?
   Der Eiffelturm

f) _____ in Düsseldorf?
   Die Königsallee

Aufgabe 10

Use all the information in Chapter 10 to answer the following questions.

a) Wie heißt die eleganteste Straße in Wien?

_____

b) Ist Düsseldorf eine schöne Stadt?

_____

c) An welchem Fluß liegt Wien?

_____

d) Wo liegt der Drachenfels?

_____

e) Wo in der Schweiz kann man Sonntags Lebensmittel kaufen?

_____

Role-plays

Kapitel 1

Besuch aus Deutschland

Character 1

a) Use the question prompts to find out about characters 2, 3 and 4.
  z.B. Character 1: Wie heißen Sie?
      Character 2: Ich heiße Hans Schulz . . .
(See also pages 2–3 of the coursebook.)

b) Use the prompts to answer questions from characters 2, 3 and 4.

a) Questions	**b) Answers**
Name?	Pierre Lebrun
Nationality?	French
Place of residence?	Live in Toulouse
Profession?	Engineer at Viard's
Married?	Married
Children?	One daughter
Learning German?	Learn German and English
Spell your name?	

- ✂

Kapitel 1

Besuch aus Deutschland

Character 2

a) Use the question prompts to find out about characters 1, 3 and 4.
  z.B. Character 2: Wie heißen Sie?
      Character 1: Ich heiße Pierre Lebrun.
(See also pages 2–3 of the coursebook.)

b) Use the prompts to answer questions from characters 1, 3 and 4.

a) Questions	**b) Answers**
Name?	Hans Schulz
Nationality?	American
Place of residence?	Live in New York
Profession?	Sales manager at Quayle & Co
Married?	Married
Children?	One son
Learning German?	Learn German at work
Spell your name?	

Kapitel 1

Besuch aus Deutschland

Character 3

a) Use the question prompts to find out about characters 1, 2 and 4.
    z.B. Character 3:   **Wie heißen Sie?**
          Character 4:   **Ich heiße Bruce Foster.**
    (See also pages 2-3 of the coursebook.)

b) Use the prompts to answer questions from characters 1, 2 and 4.

a) Questions	b) Answers
Name?	Maria Pacitto
Nationality?	Italian
Place of residence?	Live in Milan
Profession?	Student
Married?	Single
Children?	Learn German at university
Learning German?	
Spell your name?	

- ✂

Kapitel 1

Besuch aus Deutschland

Character 4

a) Use the question prompts to find out about characters 1, 2 and 3.
    z.B. Character 4:   **Wie heißen Sie?**
          Character 3:   **Ich heiße Maria Pacitto.**
    (See also pages 2-3 of the coursebook.)

b) Use the prompts to answer questions from characters 1, 2 and 3.

a) Questions	b) Answers
Name?	Bruce Foster
Nationality?	Australian
Place of residence?	Live in Melbourne
Profession?	Chief buyer at Kanga Sport
Married?	Unmarried
Children?	Learn German at home
Learning German?	
Spell your name?	

Kapitel 2

Wann fahren Sie?

Character 1

a) Use the question prompts to find out about characters 2, 3 and 4.
z.B. Character 1: Wann kommen Sie nach Deutschland?
    Character 2: Ich komme am 28. April nach Deutschland.
(See also pages 14–15 of the coursebook.)

b) Use the prompts to answer questions from characters 2, 3 and 4.

a) Questions

When to Germany?

When arriving at the airport?

Flying from Gatwick?

How long are you staying?

Book hotel room?

Double/single room?

Bath/shower?

Meet you at the airport?

b) Answers

To Germany on November 4th

Arriving at 15.30 at the airport

Flying from Heathrow

Staying three days

Single room and bath please

Please meet me at the airport at 15.45

Kapitel 2

Wann fahren Sie?

Character 2

a) Use the question prompts to find out about characters 1, 3 and 4.
z.B. Character 2: Wann kommen Sie nach Deutschland?
    Character 1: Ich komme am 4. November nach Deutschland.
(See also pages 14–15 of the coursebook.)

b) Use the prompts to answer questions from characters 1, 3 and 4.

a) Questions

When to Germany?

When arriving at the airport?

Flying from Gatwick?

How long are you staying?

Book hotel room?

Double/single room?

Bath/shower?

Meet you at the airport?

b) Answers

To Germany on April 28th

Arriving at 10.15 at the airport

Flying from Manchester

Wife is coming too – please book double room and shower

Staying four days

Please meet me at 10.30 at the airport

Kapitel 2

Wann fahren Sie?

Character 3

a) Use the question prompts to find out about characters 1, 2 and 4.
z.B. Character 3:   **Wann kommen Sie nach Deutschland?**
        Character 4:   **Ich komme am 1. Februar nach Deutschland.**
(See also pages 14–15 of the coursebook.)

b) Use the prompts to answer questions from characters 1, 2 and 4.

a) Questions	**b) Answers**
When to Germany?	To Germany on July 11th
When arriving at the airport?	Arriving at 17.00 at the airport
Flying from Gatwick?	Flying from Gatwick
How long are you staying?	Staying two days
Book hotel room?	Single room and shower please
Double/single room?	Train at 17.30 to town, please meet me at the station at 18.45
Bath/shower?	
Meet you at the airport?	

Kapitel 2

Wann fahren Sie?

Character 4

a) Use the question prompts to find out about characters 1, 2 and 3.
z.B. Character 4:   **Wann kommen Sie nach Deutschland?**
        Character 3:   **Ich komme am 11. Juli nach Deutschland.**
(See also pages 14–15 of the coursebook.)

b) Use the prompts to answer questions from characters 1, 2 and 3.

a) Questions	**b) Answers**
When to Germany?	To Germany on 1st February
When arriving at the airport?	Arriving at 12.45 at the airport
Flying from Gatwick?	Flying from Heathrow
How long are you staying?	Staying five days
Book hotel room?	Single room with bath please
Double/single room?	Please meet me at 13.00 at the airport
Bath/shower?	
Meet you at the airport?	

Unterwegs

Fahrplan

Richtung	ab	an	erster Klasse		zweiter Klasse		Gleis	Umsteigen
			→	→ ←	→	→ ←		
Bremen	9.00	12.00	DM 95	DM 180	DM 70	DM 130	7	—
	10.00	13.00						
	11.00	14.00						
	usw.							
Hannover	8.30	11.00	DM 86	DM 160	DM 64	DM 120	3	—
	9.00	11.30						
	9.30	12.00						
	usw.							
Hamburg	8.00	11.45	DM 120	DM 235	DM 100	DM 190	2	Hannover
	10.00	13.45						
	12.00	15.45						
	usw.							
Gottingen	9.20	10.30	DM 80	DM 155	DM 65	DM 120	8	Kassel
	10.20	11.30						
	11.20	12.30						
	usw.							

Kapitel 3

Unterwegs

Fahrplan

Richtung	ab	an	erster Klasse		zweiter Klasse		Gleis	Umsteigen
			→	→ ←	→	→ ←		
Bremen	9.00	12.00	DM 95	DM 180	DM 70	DM 130	7	—
	10.00	13.00						
	11.00	14.00						
	usw.							
Hannover	8.30	11.00	DM 86	DM 160	DM 64	DM 120	3	—
	9.00	11.30						
	9.30	12.00						
	usw.							
Hamburg	8.00	11.45	DM 120	DM 235	DM 100	DM 190	2	Hannover
	10.00	13.45						
	12.00	15.45						
	usw.							
Gottingen	9.20	10.30	DM 80	DM 155	DM 65	DM 120	8	Kassel
	10.20	11.30						
	11.20	12.30						
	usw.							

Unterwegs

Character 1

a) Use the question prompts and the timetable to serve passengers 2, 3 and 4. Do not let the passengers see the timetable.

   z.B. Passenger 2:   **Wann fährt der nächste Zug nach Hannover?**

         Railway clerk 1:   **Um...**

   (See also page 33 of the coursebook.)

b) Use the prompts to get information and to answer questions from clerks 2, 3 and 4.

a) Railway clerk 1	**b) Passenger 1**
First/second class?	Next train to Bremen?
Single/return?	Two single tickets
	Second-class
	Price?
	Direct?
	Platform?
	When in Bremen?

✂

Unterwegs

Character 2

a) Use the question prompts and the timetable to serve passengers 1, 3 and 4. Do not let the passengers see the timetable.

   z.B. Passenger 1:   **Wann fährt der nächste Zug nach Bremen?**

         Railway clerk 2:   **Um...**

   (See also page 33 of the coursebook.)

b) Use the prompts to get information and to answer questions from clerks 1, 3 and 4.

a) Railway clerk 2	**b) Passenger 2**
First/second class?	Next train to Hannover?
Single/return?	One return ticket first-class
	Price?
	Direct?
	Platform?
	When in Hannover?

Unterwegs

Character 3

a) Use the question prompts and the timetable to serve passengers 1, 2 and 4. Do not let the passengers see the timetable.

z.B. Passenger 4:   **Wann fährt der nächste Zug nach Göttingen?**

Railway clerk 3:   **Um . . .**

(See also page 33 of the coursebook.)

b) Use the prompts to get information and to answer questions from clerks 1, 2 and 4.

a) Railway clerk 3	**b) Passenger 3**
First/second class?	Next train to Hamburg?
Single/return?	Three return tickets
	Second-class
	Price?
	Direct?
	Platform?
	When in Hamburg?

---- ✂

Unterwegs

Character 4

a) Use the question prompts and the timetable to serve passengers 1, 2 and 3. Do not let the passengers see the timetable.

z.B. Passenger 3:   **Wann fährt der nächste Zug nach Hamburg?**

Railway clerk 4:   **Um . . .**

(See also page 33 of the coursebook.)

b) Use the prompts to get information and to answer questions from clerks 1, 2 and 3.

a) Railway clerk 4	**b) Passenger 4**
First/second class?	Next train to Göttingen?
Single/return?	One single ticket
	First-class
	Price?
	Direct?
	Platform?
	When in Göttingen?

Unterkunft in Deutschland

Character 1

a) Use the prompts to serve hotel guests 2, 3 and 4.
z.B. Receptionist 1:   Haben Sie eine Reservierung?
        Hotel guest 2:   Leider nicht . . .
(See also the conversations on pages 44–5 of the coursebook.)

b) Use the prompts to have conversations with receptionists 2, 3 and 4.

a) Receptionist 1	**b) Hotel guest 1**
Booking?	Booking – yes
Nights?	Single room with shower
Business trip?	Two nights
Complete the registration form!	Business trip – yes
Full board?	Half board
Car park – yes	Car park?
Evening meal 19.00–21.30	When is evening meal?
Single rooms – second floor	Nice view?
Double rooms – first floor	
All rooms – nice view	

Unterkunft in Deutschland

Character 2

a) Use the prompts to serve hotel guests 1, 3 and 4.
z.B. Receptionist 2:   Haben Sie eine Reservierung?
        Hotel guest 1:   Ja, ich habe ein Einzelzimmer mit Dusche reserviert.
(See also the conversations on pages 44–5 of the coursebook.)

b) Use the prompts to have conversations with receptionists 1, 3 and 4.

a) Receptionist 2	**b) Hotel guest 2**
Booking?	Booking – no, rooms free?
Nights?	Double room with bath
Business trip?	One night
Complete the registration form!	Business – no, holiday
Full board?	Bed and breakfast
Car park – yes, small	Car park?
Evening meal 19.30–22.00	When is evening meal?
All rooms – view over park	Nice view?

Unterkunft in Deutschland

Character 3

a) Use the prompts to serve hotel guests 1, 2 and 4.
z.B. Receptionist 3:   Haben Sie ein Zimmer reserviert?
       Hotel guest 4:   Ja, ich habe ein Einzelzimmer mit Bad reserviert.
(See also the conversations on pages 44–5 of the coursebook.)

b) Use the prompts to have conversations with receptionists 1, 2 and 4.

a) Receptionist 3	**b) Hotel guest 3**
Booking?	Booking – yes
Nights?	Two single rooms with baths
Business trip?	Balcony and TV
Complete the registration form!	Three nights
Full board?	Business – no, holiday
Car park – behind hotel	Full board – yes
Evening meal 18.00–21.00	Car park?
All rooms – nice view	When is evening meal?
	Nice view?

- ✂ - - -

Unterkunft in Deutschland

Character 4

a) Use the prompts to serve hotel guests 1, 2 and 3.
z.B. Receptionist 4:   Haben Sie ein Zimmer reserviert?
       Hotel guest 3:   Ja, wir haben zwei Einzelzimmer mit Bad reserviert.
(See also the conversations on pages 44–5 of the coursebook.)

b) Use the prompts to have conversations with receptionists 1, 2 and 3.

a) Receptionist 4	**b) Hotel guest 4**
Booking?	Booking – yes
Nights?	One single room with bath
Business trip?	One night
Complete the registration form!	Business – yes
Full board?	Half board
Car park – no, park in the street	Car park?
Evening meal 18.30–22.00	When is evening meal?
Double rooms–view of river	Nice view?
Single rooms–view of mountains	

Essen und Trinken

Character 1 (role-play 1)

a) Use the prompts to serve diner 2.
z.B. Waiter 1:   Was darf es sein?
      Diner 2:   Wir möchten einen Tisch für vier Personen, bitte.
(See also the conversations on pages 58-9 of the coursebook.)

b) Use the prompts to have a conversation with waiter 2.

a) Waiter 1

Can I help you?

Table by the window?

Chosen?

Dessert?

Drink?

Bill (use the prices on the menu)

b) Diner 1

Table for three please

Menu/drinks list please

Starter – no

Main course – what do you recommend?

Dessert – yes

Wine

Bill please, must leave right away

Kapitel 5

Essen und Trinken

Character 2 (role-play 1)

a) Use the prompts to serve diner 1.
z.B. Waiter 2:   Was darf es sein?
      Diner 1:   Wir möchten einen Tisch für drei Personen, bitte.
(See also the conversations on pages 58-9 of the coursebook.)

b) Use the prompts to have a conversation with waiter 1.

a) Waiter 2

Can I help you?

Table in the corner

Chosen?

Dessert?

Drink?

Bill (use the prices on the menu)

b) Diner 2

Table for four please

Menu please

Starter – yes

Main course – not fish

Dessert – yes

Beer

71

Kapitel 5

Essen und Trinken

Character 1 (role-play 2)

a) Use the prompts to have a conversation with guest 2.
z.B. Host 1:   Haben Sie gut geschlafen?
Guest 2:   Ja, ganz gut danke...
(See also the conversations on pages 56–7 of the coursebook.)

b) Use the prompts to have a conversation with host 2.

a) Host 1

Sleep well?

Good journey?

First time in Düsseldorf?

Already met Mr Walter?

See the sights?

b) Guest 1

Sleep well – yes

Good journey – yes

Hotel very comfortable

First time here – no

Last year on business met Mr Walter at a trade fair in Frankfurt in May

See the sights – yes please

Not much time last year

-- ✂

Kapitel 5

Essen und Trinken

Character 2 (role-play 2)

a) Use the prompts to have a conversation with guest 1.
z.B. Host 2:   Haben Sie gut geschlafen?
Guest 1:   Ja, sehr gut danke...
(See also the conversations on pages 56–7 of the coursebook.)

b) Use the prompts to have a conversation with host 1.

a) Host 2

Sleep well?

Good journey?

First time in Düsseldorf?

Already met Mr Walter?

See the sights?

b) Guest 2

Slept quite well

Journey – good

Hotel – very nice

First visit

Don't know Mr Walter, met his colleague Mr Jung in London in January

See the sights – yes please

Heard a lot about Düsseldorf

Essen und Trinken

Speisekarte

Vorspeisen

	DM
Salatteller mit Crevetten, Geflügelstreifen, Brot und Butter	16.50
Crevetten mit feinem Cointreau Orangendressing, Weißbrot und Butter	16.50

Warme Gerichte

Gebackene Auberginen mit Pommes Duchesse	10.50
Schweinesteak in Majorammantel, Rotweinsauce, Croquetten und Salat	19.50
Filetsteak mit Schalottenpuree überbacken	27.50

Kalte Gerichte

2 Matjesfilets "Hausfrauen Art"	12.50
Kalter Braten mit Bratkartoffeln	13.50

Nachtisch

Potpourri von Früchten mit creme royale überbacken	9.50
Mousse von weißer Schokolade	9.80
Vanilleiscreme mit flambierten Himbeeren	14.50

Getränke

Weine

Mosel – Saar – Ruwer

Wehlener Münzlay		
Riesling	17.60	
Bernkasteler Kurfürstlay		
Kabinett	18.00	
Rüdesheimer Rosengarten	18.60	
Aßmannshäuser		
Hollenberg Spätburgunder	19.80	
Niersteiner Gutes Domtal	16.50	

Biere

König Pilsener	kleines	2.30
	großes	4.60
Dortmunder Pilsener	kleines	2.50
	großes	5.00

Mineralwasser	2.00
Fanta	2.50
Cola	2.50
Apfelsaft	3.00
Orangensaft	3.00
Tee (Tasse)	2.30
Tee (Kännchen)	4.10
Kaffee (Tasse)	2.50
Kaffee (Kännchen)	4.80
Espresso	2.80
Capuccino	3.50
Schokolade	3.10

Einkaufen

Character 1 (role-play 1)

a) Use the prompts to serve customer 2.
z.B. Sales assistant 1: **Was darf es sein?**
Customer 2:   **Ich suche eine Jacke, bitte.**
(See also the conversation on page 76 of the coursebook.)

b) Use the prompts to have a conversation with sales assistant 2. Use the chart of clothing sizes.

a) Sales assistant 1

Can I help you?

Colour?

Size?

Shirts DM 30–DM 45, all colours

Jackets DM 98–DM 180, only in dark grey or blue

Gift wrap?

b) Customer 1

Shirt please

Red

Size – for my father (brother, son etc.)

Price?

Preferably not too expensive

Gift wrap – yes please

Einkaufen

Character 2 (role-play 2)

a) Use the prompts to serve customer 1.
z.B. Sales assistant 2: **Was darf es sein?**
Customer 1:   **Ich möchte ein Hemd, bitte.**
(See also the conversation on page 76 of the coursebook.)

b) Use the prompts to have a conversation with sales assistant 1. Use the chart of clothing sizes.

a) Sales assistant 2

Can I help you?

Colour?

Size?

Shirts DM 30–DM 45, all colours

Gift wrap?

b) Customer 2

Looking for a jacket

Black

Size – for me

Price?

Can I try it on?*

(***anprobieren** sep)

It does not fit

Next size?

Kapitel 6

Einkaufen

Character 3 (role-play 2)

a) Use the prompts to serve customer 2.
   z.B. Sales assistant 1: **Was darf es sein?**
        Customer 2:   **Ich möchte ein T-shirt.**
   (See also the conversation on page 76 of the coursebook.)

b) Use the prompts to have a conversation with sales assistant 2. Use the chart of clothing sizes.

a) Sales assistant 1

Can I help you?

Colour?

Size?

Shirts DM 25–DM 50, all colours

Jackets DM 98–DM 180

T-shirts all sizes, no motif – DM 15.50, with motif – DM 18.30

Gift wrap?

b) Customer 1

Shirt please

Blue

Size – for me (my husband, uncle, father etc.)

Price?

Prefer an expensive one, better quality

May I try it on? *

(*anprobieren sep)

It fits

Kapitel 6

Einkaufen

Character 4 (role-play 2)

a) Use the prompts to serve customer 1.
   z.B. Sales assistant 2: **Was darf es sein?**
        Customer 1:   **Ich möchte ein Hemd, bitte.**
   (See also the conversation on page 76 of the coursebook.)

b) Use the prompts to have a conversation with sales assistant 1. Use the chart of clothing sizes.

a) Sales assistant 2

Can I help you?

Colour?

Size?

Shirts DM 30–DM 45, all colours

Jackets DM 98–DM 180

Gift wrap?

b) Customer 2

T-Shirt please

Mickey Mouse motif

Size – 104 cm

Yellow

For my daughter (son)

Price?

Gift wrap – yes

Women's dresses, blouses, sweaters, skirts				
British	10	12	14	16
American	8	10	12	14
French/German	36	38	40	42
Spanish/Portuguese	38	40	42	44
Italian	40	42	44	46

Men's sweaters, suits, coats
(British size = chest measurement in inches)

British & American	36	38	40	42
European	46	48	50	52

Men's shirts
(British size = neck size in inches)

British & American	15	$15\frac{1}{2}$	16	$16\frac{1}{2}$
European	38	39	40	41

Babies and Children
British and Continental Sizes

Age	Sizes in centimetres
0–6 months	70
6–12 months	80
12–18 months	86
18–24 months	92
2–3 years	98
3–4 years	104
4–5 years	110
5–6 years	116
7–8 years	128
9–10 years	134

Kapitel 6

Einkaufen

Women's dresses, blouses, sweaters, skirts				
British	10	12	14	16
American	8	10	12	14
French/German	36	38	40	42
Spanish/Portuguese	38	40	42	44
Italian	40	42	44	46

Men's sweaters, suits, coats
(British size = chest measurement in inches)

British & American	36	38	40	42
European	46	48	50	52

Men's shirts
(British size = neck size in inches)

British & American	15	$15\frac{1}{2}$	16	$16\frac{1}{2}$
European	38	39	40	41

Babies and Children
British and Continental Sizes

Age	Sizes in centimetres
0–6 months	70
6–12 months	80
12–18 months	86
18–24 months	92
2–3 years	98
3–4 years	104
4–5 years	110
5–6 years	116
7–8 years	128
9–10 years	134

Kapitel 7

Krankheit und Unfall

Character 1 (role-play 1)

a) Use the prompts to have a conversation with Mr Jones.
z.B. Doctor 1: **Was fehlt Ihnen?**
    Mr Jones: **Ich habe Ohrenschmerzen.**
(See also the conversation on pages 86-7 of the coursebook.)

b) Use the prompts to have a conversation with doctor 2.

a) Doctor 1

What is the matter?

Medical insurance record card?

How long have you had pains?

Infection

Prescription for drops

Four times a day, until pains go

Chemist's on the market place

b) Herr Schmidt

Headache and fever since yesterday, throat sore too

How often take tablets?

How long for?

Supposed to visit customers tomorrow – is that OK?

Need sick note please

Kapitel 7

Krankheit und Unfall

Character 2 (role-play 1)

a) Use the prompts to have a conversation with Herr Schmidt.
z.B. Doctor 2: **Was fehlt Ihnen?**
    Herr Schmidt: **Ich habe Kopfschmerzen und Fieber.**
(See also the conversation on pages 86-7 of the coursebook.)

b) Use the prompts to have a conversation with doctor 1.

a) Doctor 2

What is the matter?

How long have you had pains?

Flu

Prescription for tablets

Three times a day

One tablet before meals until they are all used up

Better to spend 2-3 days at home

Get well soon!

b) Mr Jones

Earache

No medical insurance record card, here on holiday so holiday insurance

Three days

How often use drops?

For how long do I use drops?

Where is the chemist's?

Krankheit und Unfall

Character 1 (role-play 2)

a) Use the prompts to serve Mr Jones.
   z.B. Chemist 1:   Bitte schön?
        Mr Jones: Ich habe hier ein Rezept vom Arzt.
   (See also the conversation on page 89 of the coursebook.)

b) Use the prompts to have a conversation with chemist 2.

a) Chemist 1

Can I help you?

I will get the drops

These are very good, I use them too

Live here/visitor?

Use the drops at once

b) Herr Schmidt

Was at the doctor's, I have a prescription

Sore throat too

Tablets with/without water?

I like whisky!

How annoying!

May I ring my wife from here? She can fetch me. I'll go straight to bed

---

Krankheit und Unfall

Character 2 (role-play 2)

a) Use the prompts to serve Herr Schmidt.
   z.B. Chemist 2:   Kann ich Ihnen helfen?
        Herr Schmidt: Ich war gerade beim Arzt.
   (See also the conversation on page 89 of the coursebook.)

b) Use the prompts to have a conversation with chemist 1.

a) Chemist 2

Can I help you?

I will get the tablets

Sore throat too?

I recommend these

Take with water – no alcohol!

Of course you may use the phone

Would you like a chair?

b) Mr Jones

Prescription from the doctor

Sorry – I can hardly hear, ears very painful

On holiday for two weeks

Thanks, perhaps I will sleep better now

Kapitel 8

Geld, Bank und Post

Character 1 (role-play 1)

a) Use the prompts to serve customer 2.
z.B. Bank clerk 1:   Bitte schön?
        Customer 2:   Ich möchte Reiseschecks einlösen.
(See also the conversations on pages 98–100 of the coursebook.)

b) Use the prompts to have a conversation with bank clerk 2.

a) Bank clerk 1

Can I help you?

Passport?

DM 2,98/£1

Please sign

Take the receipt to the cashpoint

How would you like the money?

b) Customer 1

Change cash?

DM 600 to English money

Rate of exchange?

Passport – no, identity card

10 × £20 notes and some change please
(might need change at the airport)

Kapitel 8

Geld, Bank und Post

Character 2 (role-play 1)

a) Use the prompts to serve customer 1.
z.B. Bank clerk 2:   Bitte schön?
        Customer 1:   Kann ich hier Bargeld wechseln?
(See also the conversations on pages 98–100 of the coursebook.)

b) Use the prompts to have a conversation with bank clerk 1.

a) Bank clerk 2

Can I help you?

DM 3,00/£1

Passport?

I will give you 9 × £20 notes, 1 × £10 note,
1 × £5 note and some change

Please go to the cashpoint

b) Customer 2

Change traveller's cheques please

6 × £25 cheques

Passport – yes

Rate of exchange?

Do I get the money here?

4 × DM 100 notes and some change

Geld, Bank und Post

Character 1 (role-play 2)

a) Use the prompts to serve customer 2.
    z.B. Post office clerk 1:   Bitte schön?
           Customer 2:   Ich möchte Briefmarken bitte . . .
(See also the conversations on page 102 of the coursebook.)

b) Use the prompts to have a conversation with post office clerk 2.

a) Post office clerk 1	**b) Customer 1**
Can I help you?	Stamps: 3×80 Pf., 3×50 Pf.
Anything else?	Parcel for abroad
The parcel weighs 150 g (DM 2,75)	Book – a gift
(Work out total price)	Cost DM 17,20
Postbox – in the corner	How much altogether?
	When will parcel arrive?
	3–4 days OK

Geld, Bank und Post

Character 2 (role-play 2)

a) Use the prompts to serve customer 1.
    z.B. Post office clerk 2:   Was darf es sein?
           Customer 1:   Ich möchte Briefmarken bitte . . .
(See also the conversations on page 102 of the coursebook.)

b) Use the prompts to have a conversation with post office clerk 1.

a) Post office clerk 2	**b) Customer 2**
Can I help you?	Stamps: 3×80 Pf., 2×50 Pf.
Anything else?	Parcel – inland
Fill in form, is it a present?	How much altogether?
How much was it?	Where do I post the letters?
Parcel costs DM 4,50	
(Work out total price)	
Parcel should take 3–4 days	

Kapitel 9

Auto und Zoll

Character 1 (role-play 1)

a) Use the prompts to serve customer 2.
    z.B. Garage attendant 1: **Bitte schön?**
          Customer 2:   **Volltanken bitte.**
    (See also the conversation on page 112 of the coursebook.)

b) Use the prompts to have a conversation with garage attendant 2.

a) Garage attendant 1

Can I help you?

Super/normal?

Anything else?

Top up water?

DM 48 altogether

Please pay at the cash desk

Receipt – of course! Have a good trip!

b) Customer 1

20 litres lead-free, normal please

Please check the oil

How much?

How do I get to the motorway for Cologne?

- ✂

Kapitel 9

Auto und Zoll

Character 2 (role-play 1)

a) Use the prompts to serve customer 1.
    z.B. Garage attendant 2: **Was darf es sein?**
          Customer 1:   **Ich hätte gern 20 Liter bleifrei.**
    (See also the conversation on page 112 of the coursebook.)

b) Use the prompts to have a conversation with garage attendant 1.

a) Garage attendant 2

Can I help you?

Anything else?

Oil – OK

DM 35 please

Go down here – you have got the right of way,
turn right at the traffic lights

b) Customer 2

Fill it up please!

Super – unleaded

Check the tyre pressure please

Water OK, just topped up this morning

How much?

Where do I pay?

Receipt please!

Auto und Zoll

Character 1 (role-play 2)

a) Use the prompts to have a conversation with driver 2.
  z.B. Customs officer 1:   **Ihre Papiere bitte.**
        Driver 2:   **Bitte schön.**
  (See also the conversation on page 109 of the coursebook.)

b) Use the prompts to have a conversation with customs officer 2.

a) Customs officer 1

May I see your papers?

Where are you going?

Anything to declare?

Unfortunately have to search your vehicle, random check – only 5–10 minutes

Parking place round the corner

b) Driver 1

Here you are!

Düsseldorf

Visiting customers – appointment in $2\frac{1}{2}$ hours, will I manage it?

Will not drive faster than 130 km per hour – I don't want to have an accident

- -

Auto und Zoll

Character 2 (role-play 2)

a) Use the prompts to have a conversation with driver 1.
  z.B. Customs officer 2:   **Darf ich Ihre Papiere sehen?**
        Driver 1:   **Bitte schön.**
  (See also the conversation on page 109 of the coursebook.)

b) Use the prompts to have a conversation with customs officer 1.

a) Customs officer 2

Papers please!

Everything is in order

Where are you going?

Düsseldorf – possible, not a lot of traffic today, but don't drive too fast!

b) Driver 2

Here you are!

Rotterdam, then overnight ferry to Hull

Nothing to declare

Please be quick, the ferry leaves at 18.00 and I must be at the port by 17.00

Kapitel 10

Stadtbesichtigung und Freizeit

Revision

Can you answer these questions about your job and travels to date?

Arbeit

Was sind Sie von Beruf?

Bei welcher Firma arbeiten Sie?

Wie lange arbeiten Sie schon da?

Können Sie Ihre Arbeit auf Deutsch beschreiben?

Wie fahren Sie jeden Tag zur Arbeit?

Hat Ihre Firma Vertreter oder Kunden in Deutschland?

Müssen Sie manchmal Geschäftsreisen ins Ausland machen? Wenn ja, wohin?

Reisen

Welche Länder haben Sie besucht?

Geschäftsreise/Urlaub?

Sind Sie geflogen? Wenn ja, von welchem Flughafen sind Sie abgeflogen?

Wer hat Sie im Ausland vom Flughafen abgeholt?

Sind Sie mit dem Schiff nach Holland, Belgien oder Frankreich gefahren?

Haben Sie Ihr eigenes Auto mitgenommen?

Mußten Sie etwas verzollen?

Haben die Zollbeamten Ihr Auto durchsucht?

Ist es schwierig, rechts zu fahren?

Mußten Sie oft volltanken?

Welche Sehenswürdigkeiten haben Sie gesehen?

Haben Sie Reiseschecks mitgenommen?

Wo haben Sie Geld gewechselt?

Wie war der Wechselkurs?

Sind Kleider, Essen und Trinken billiger oder teurer in anderen europäischen Ländern?

Sind Sie mit dem Zug ins Ausland gefahren?

Haben Sie einen Fahrausweisautomaten benutzt?

Mußten Sie umsteigen?

Wie lange hat die Reise gedauert?

Können Sie die Reise beschreiben?

Unterkunft

Haben Sie im Ausland in einem Hotel oder in einem Gasthaus übernachtet?

Wie war das Hotel oder der Gasthof? (bequem, teuer . . .)

Haben Sie bei Freunden/Bekannten gewohnt?

Wie haben Sie Ihre Bekannten kennengelernt?

Haben Sie einen Campingplatz im Ausland benutzt?

Allgemeines

Was für Geschenke haben Sie nach Hause gebracht?

Wie hat Ihnen das Essen und Trinken im Ausland geschmeckt?

Haben Sie deutsch oder eine andere Fremdsprache gesprochen?
Haben Sie Kollegen/Kunden oder andere Leute kennengelernt?

Freizeit
Was machen Sie gern in Ihrer Freizeit?
Wenn Sie z.B. gern Golf spielen, können Sie auf Deutsch erklären, wie man Golf spielt?
Wenn Sie gern ins Theater oder ins Kino gehen – was ist das interessanteste Theaterstück oder der beste/schlechteste Film den Sie gesehen haben?
Können Sie die Geschichte auf Deutsch erzählen?

Vocabulary lists

Kapitel 1

Besuch aus Deutschland

Aufenthalt (-e) m	stay	Kind (-er) n	child
Beruf (-e) m	profession	Mal (-e) n	time
Deutsche (-n) m	German (man)		
Engländer (-) m	Englishman	arbeiten	to work
Franzose (-n) m	Frenchman	buchstabieren	to spell
Geschäftsführer (-) m	managing director	erwarten	to expect
Italiener (-) m	Italian (man)	freuen (refl)	to be pleased
Mann (¨er) m	man, husband	haben	to have
Name (-n) m	name	heißen	to be called
Produktionsleiter (-) m	production manager	kennen lernen	to get to know, meet
Sohn (¨e) m	son	kommen	to come
Tag (-e) m	day	sein	to be
Vater (¨) m	father	sprechen	to speak, talk
Verkaufsleiter (-) m	sales manager	studieren	to study
Vertreter (-) m	representative	wohnen	to live
Waliser (-) m	Welshman	wünschen	to wish
Firma (Firmen) f	firm, company		
Frau (-en) f	woman, wife	auch	also, too
Mutter (¨) f	mother	deutsch	German
Schule (-n) f	school	englisch	English
Sekretärin (-nen) f	secretary	französisch	French
Staatsangehörigkeit (-en) f	nationality	gleich	at once
		hier	here
Tochter (¨) f	daughter	italienisch	Italian
Universität (-en) f	university	oft	often
Verkaufsleiterin (-nen) f	female sales manager	selbst	myself
		vielleicht	perhaps

Kapitel 2

Wann fahren Sie?

Augenblick (-e) m	moment	Dusche (-n) f	shower
Bahnhof (¨e) m	railway station	Hilfe (-n) f	help
Besuch (-e) m	visit	Messe (-n) f	trade fair
Dom (-e) m	cathedral	Stadt (¨e) f	town
Flughafen (¨) m	airport	Uhr (-en) f	watch, clock
Januar m	January		
Montag m	Monday	Bad (¨er) n	bath
Zug (¨e) m	train	Flugzeug (-e) n	aeroplane
		Hotel (-s) n	hotel
Autobahn (-en) f	motorway	Zimmer (-) n	room
Bahn (-en) f	rail		

abfliegen (sep)	to fly from	möchten	would like to
abholen (sep)	to meet, pick up	reservieren	to reserve, book
ankommen (sep)	to arrive	sollen	should, ought
besuchen	to visit	verbinden	to connect
bleiben	to stay		
empfehlen	to recommend		
fahren	to go, travel (not on foot)	bald	soon
		für (acc)	for
fliegen	to fly	von (dat)	from

Kapitel 3

Unterwegs

Automat (-en) m	automatic machine	Geld (-er) n	money
Beamte (die Beamten) m	official	Gleis (-e) n	platform
		Mitglied (er) n	member
Fahrpreis (-e) m	travel cost	Ziel (-e) n	destination
Schalter (-) m	counter		
Abfahrt (-en) f	departure	abfahren (sep)	to leave, depart
Ankunft (-e) f	arrival	bekommen	to get
Auskunft (-e) f	information	einsteigen (sep)	to get into, board
Fahrkarte (-n) f	ticket	entwerten	to cancel, stamp
Klasse (-n) f	class	stempeln	to stamp
Rolltreppe (-n) f	escalator	umsteigen (sep)	to change (transport)
Taste (-n) f	push-button, key	wechseln	to change (money)

Kapitel 4

Unterkunft in Deutschland

Balkon (-s) m	balcony	Jugendherberge (-n) f	youth hostel
Berg (-e) m	mountain	Sehenswürdigkeit (-en) f	places of interest
Fahrstuhl (-e) m	lift		
Fluß (Flüsse) m	river	Umgebung (-en) f	area
Garten (-) m	garden	Unterkunft (-e) f	accommodation
Parkplatz (-e) m	car park	Vollpension f	full board
Schlüssel (-) m	key		
Stadtrand (-er) m	edge of town, outskirts	Abendessen (-) n	dinner, evening meal
Stock (-e) m	floor, storey	Anmeldeformular (-e) n	registration form
Aussicht (-en) f	view	Eßzimmer (-) n	dining room
Ecke (-n) f	corner	Fernsehen (-) n	television
Halbpension f	half board	Frühstück (-e) n	breakfast

Gepäck n	luggage
Schlafzimmer (-) n	bedroom
ausfüllen (sep)	to fill out, complete
besichtigen	to look round
nehmen	to take
sehen	to see
stimmen	to be right

angenehm (adj)	pleasant
billig	cheap
erstklassig	first-class
niedrig	low
ruhig	quiet
sonnig	sunny
teuer	expensive

Kapitel 5

Essen und Trinken

Bekannte (-n) m/f	acquaintance
Gesamtbetrag (¨e) m	total amount
Nachtisch (-e) m	dessert
Pfannkuchen (-) m	pancake
Rotkohl m	red cabbage
Sauerbraten m	pickled beef
Erbse (-n) f	pea
Flasche (-n) f	bottle
Herrschaften (pl)	ladies and gentlemen
Kartoffel (-n) f	potato
Rechnung (-en) f	bill, account
Reise (-n) f	journey
Speisekarte (-n) f	menu
Suppe (-n) f	soup
Vorspeise (-n) f	hors d'oeuvre
Apfelkompott n	stewed apple
Eis (-) n	ice cream

Gemüse (pl) n	vegetables
Hauptgericht (-e) n	main course
bestellen	to order
essen	to eat
hören	to hear
schlafen	to sleep
schmecken (dat)	to taste
trinken	to drink
wählen	to choose
ausreichend	sufficient, ample
berühmt	famous
lecker	delicious
mehrere	several
müde	tired
verschieden	various, different
zahlreich	numerous

Kapitel 6

Einkaufen

Frühling m	Spring
Herbst m	Autumn
Sommer m	Summer
Spaziergang (¨e) m	walk
Verkehrsverein (-e) m	Tourist Office
Winter m	Winter
Abteilung (-en) f	department
Bekleidung f	clothing
Farbe (-n) f	colour
Gasse (-n) f	alley

Größe (-n) f	size
Kreuzung (-en) f	crossroads
Steuer (-n) f	tax
Umrechnungstabelle (-n) f	conversion table
Andenken (-) n	souvenir
Einkommen (-) n	income
Geschäft (-e) n	shop
Geschenk (-e) n	present
Spielzeug (-e) n	toy

einkaufen (sep)	to shop	entlang	along
gefallen (dat)	to please	gelb	yellow
kriegen	to get	geradeaus	straight on
passen (dat)	to fit	links	on the left
wissen	to know	rechts	on the right
		rot	red
bestimmt	certainly	schwarz	black
blau	blue	verschieden	different
braun	brown	weiß	white

Kapitel 7

Krankheit und Unfall

Durchfall m	diarrhoea	Sprechstundenhilfe (–n) f	doctor's receptionist
Hals (⏜e) m	throat		
Kopf (⏜e) m	head		
Krankenschein (–e) m	medical insurance card	Herz (–en) n	heart
Mund (⏜er) m	mouth	Magenweh n	stomach ache
Rücken (–) m	back	Ohr (–en) n	ear
Schmerz (–en) m	pain	Rezept (–e) n	prescription
Termin (–e) m	appointment		
Zahn (⏜e) m	tooth	aufbrauchen (sep)	to use up
Apotheke (–n) f	chemist's shop	einnehmen (sep)	to take (medicine)
Grippe f	flu	fehlen (dat)	to be the matter
Krankenversicherung f	health insurance	nachlassen (sep)	to abate, cease
Sprechstunden (pl) f	surgery hours	weiterzahlen (sep)	to continue paying

---

Kapitel 8

Geld, Bank und Post

Betrieb (–e) m	company	Postleitzahl (–en) f	post code
Einlieferungsschein (–e) m	certificate of posting	Verbindung (–en) f	connection
Fernmeldeingenieur (–e) m	post office engineer	Bargeld n	cash
		Kleingeld n	change
Kurs (–e) m	exchange rate	Konto (Konten) n	account
Paß (Pässe) m	passport	Paket (–e) n	parcel
Personalausweis (–e) m	identity card	Postamt (⏜er) n	post office
Reisescheck (–s) m	traveller's cheque	Postwertzeichen (–) n	postage stamp
Schein (–e) m	note (money)	abheben	to take out (money from account)
Bundesdruckerei f	federal printing works	einlösen (sep)	to cash
Bundespost f	federal postal service	einwerfen (sep)	to put, post
Geheimzahl (–en) f	secret number	wechseln	to change, exchange
Herstellung f	production	knapp	just under

Kapitel 9

Auto und Zoll

Beleg (-e) m	voucher
Führerschein (-e) m	driving licence
Luftdruck m	tyre pressure
Ölstand m	oil level
Reifendruck m	tyre pressure
Zollbeamte (-n) m	customs officer
Bremse (-n) f	brake
Grenze (-n) f	border
Höchstgeschwindig- keit (-en)	top speed
Panne (-n) f	breakdown
Stichprobe (-n) f	random check
Tankstelle (-n) f	petrol station
Versicherungskarte (-n) f	insurance card
Vorfahrt f	right of way
Benzin n	petrol
Fahrzeug (-e) n	vehicle
Gewicht (-e) n	weight
Nachtschiff (-e) n	overnight ferry
durchsuchen	to search
nachfüllen (sep)	to top up
prüfen	to test, check
schaffen	to manage
verbrauchen	to use, consume
verzollen	to declare (customs)
volltanken (sep)	to fill up (with petrol)
ärgerlich	annoying

Kapitel 10

Stadtbesichtigung und Freizeit

Auftrag (¨e) m	order, commission
Geschäftsmann (-leute) m	businessman
Griff (-e) m	handle
Heimarbeiter (-) m	people who work at home
Löffel (-) m	spoon
Stahl m	steel
Fußgängerzone (-n) f	pedestrian precinct
Gegenwart f	present time
Kunstgalerie (-n) f	art gallery
Rufnummer (-n) f	telephone number
Schere (-n) f	scissors
Erlebnis (-se) n	experience
Gebäude (-) n	building
Messer (-) n	knife
Schneidgerät (-e) n	cutting implement
Schwert (-er) n	sword
Stadtviertel (-) n	part of town
Ufer (-) n	river bank
beschäftigen	to employ
besichtigen	to look round
verbringen	to spend time
versäumen	to miss
nützlich	useful
rostfrei	stainless
unbedingt	definitely
weltbekannt	world famous

Other business language books from Stanley Thornes:

M Mitchell *Working with French* (Coursebooks, Teacher's Books, Cassettes)
S Oudot *Guide to Correspondence in French*
T Connell and J Kattán-Ibarra *Working with Spanish* (Coursebooks, Teacher's Notes, Cassettes)
T Connell and J Kattán-Ibarra *Spanish at Work* (Coursebook, Teacher's Book, Cassettes)
M Jackson *Guide to Correspondence in Spanish*
D Aust and C Shepherd *Lettere Sigillatte*